Complete Planning Permission

How to get it, stop it or alter it

Roy Speer and Mike Dade

About the authors

Roy Speer and Mike Dade are Chartered Planning and
Development Surveyors who have run their own practice,
Speer Dade Planning Consultants, since 1991. They specialize
in getting planning permission and protecting property from
harmful development, working throughout the country for
private individuals and businesses on a wide range of projects,
with an emphasis on residential development. In addition, they
write regularly for magazines and speak on planning issues.
Roy and Mike are authors of *How to Get Planning Permission*,
How to Find and Buy a Building Plot and *How to Stop and
Influence Planning Permission*.

Acknowledgements

Figure 6.1 is reproduced under the terms of an Open Government
Licence. Figures 6.4 and 6.5 are reproduced with kind permission
of Woolhampton Design Centre.

Complete Planning Permission

How to get it, stop it or alter it

Roy Speer and Mike Dade

Also available in ebook

Contents

Disclaimer

The authors, publishers and their assigns make no
representation, express or implied, with regard to the accuracy
of the information contained in this publication and cannot
accept any responsibility in law for any errors or omissions. The
information in this publication contains general guidelines only
and does not represent to be advice on any particular matter
or project. No reader, purchaser or other third party should
act on the basis of material or information contained in this
publication without first taking professional advice appropriate
to their particular circumstances.

How to use this book

The Teach Yourself Breakthrough series has a number of features to help you get the most out of reading this book. *Complete Planning Permission* includes the following boxed features:

 Key idea boxes distil the most important ideas and thoughts.

 Remember this boxes contain useful tips, and help you to take away what really matters.

 Focus points are the key things you should remember from that chapter.

 The **next step** introduces you to the subject that follows.

Introduction

The UK planning system has existed for over 60 years and in that time has steadily grown in scope and complexity. Despite its importance in shaping our physical environment, it is widely misunderstood and misrepresented in the media. Not surprisingly, then, the planning process remains something of a mystery to most members of the public who have never had to deal with it and is, often, equally baffling to many who have. Yet it can be of vital significance to all householders wishing to improve or build their homes and to everyone trying to protect their neighbourhood.

For the first time, *Complete Planning Permission* brings together all aspects of the planning system in one book. It is arranged in three parts: the first outlines the planning system and how planning decisions are made; the second deals with making applications; and the third concerns objecting to applications made by others. Whether you are trying to obtain planning permission or to stop it, this book tells you, in practical terms, exactly how to go about it. Once you know where to go for information and what to do and when, the planning system becomes a great deal more useable.

Armed with this book you can confidently and effectively make planning applications or object to ones which adversely affect your interests. Importantly, it also alerts you to the situations where you are most likely to need professional help, which this book is not intended to replace. With the system continually evolving in the light of appeal and court decisions, coupled with changes to legislation and regulations, we recommend you take professional advice, where necessary, on the specific circumstances of your case. With a good understanding of the system, you will be well-placed to ensure you get the right advice, from the right people, to best advance your cause.

The planning system is similar in the four countries of the United Kingdom but they are covered by separate laws, rules and policy. *Complete Planning Permission* is based on the system in England, although it draws attention to some important differences in rules and terminology in the other countries.

PART 1

THE PLANNING SYSTEM

The nature of planning

In this chapter you will learn:

▶ *What the planning system does and why it was introduced*

▶ *How planning policy underpins the planning system*

▶ *About the different types of applications and consents*

▶ *About appeals against decisions*

▶ *How local authorities can deal with breaches of planning regulations*

What the system does

In 1948 the right to carry out property development was nationalized. In other words, landowners' right to build and alter buildings, or to use land or buildings for a different purpose, was taken away by the government. Since that date, anyone wishing to carry out development needs permission to do so. Permission is given mainly by the local planning authority for the area, which in most cases is the district, borough or city council (collectively referred to as 'district' councils). In addition, local government was charged with preparing plans for their areas showing where various kinds of buildings could and could not be built. Thus, the modern comprehensive planning system was born.

The system is now overseen by Department of Communities and Local Government in England; the Scottish Government; the Welsh Assembly Government and the Department of the Environment in Northern Ireland.

Key idea

Most new buildings and changes of use need planning permission.

The planning system was introduced so that property development could be controlled in the public interest. Previously, buildings could be built anywhere, or they could be demolished, and land and buildings could be used for any purpose the owner chose. This was thought to be inefficient and sometimes had harmful consequences. The idea behind the planning system is that new buildings and uses are controlled to ensure:

- that incompatible uses are not sited together;
- the preservation of important buildings and areas;
- the conservation of the countryside and natural environment;
- the prevention of urban sprawl;
- that the appearance and layout of new development is compatible with existing development;

- that resources are not wasted;
- that infrastructure can be provided efficiently;
- that people's enjoyment of their properties is protected;
- highway safety;
- co-ordinated provision of new housing and employment facilities.

However, the planning system is not coercive. It relies on landowners wanting to undertake development. An owner does not have to use land in a particular way just because it is allocated for that use or development. Similarly, even when permission is given, the owner is not compelled to act on it.

The system is only concerned with what can be built. It does not deal with how it is built. Structural stability, health and safety, sanitation and so on are dealt with under separate legislation and regulations.

Role of planning policy

Fundamental to the planning system is planning policy. As well as allocating sites and areas for certain types of development, council development plans contain guidance and standards for buildings and uses, relating to matters such as design, layout, density, garden space, privacy, noise, highway safety, size and mix of buildings, parking and many other issues. This guidance, and standards, is known as planning policy and can be set out in a range of development plan documents. There is a preparation process that development plans must go through and public consultation and opportunities for public comment are built into the procedures.

Key idea

Planning decisions are based primarily on planning policies.

In addition to local policies, the governments of the UK publish national planning policy documents. Inevitably, these are more broad-brush in nature. Their function is not only to guide decisions on individual development proposals but also to give direction to the development plans drawn up by local authorities. The government indicates what should be taken into account when preparing local plans and, in some areas, the thrust of what they should say.

When seeking permission for development, planning law requires the body responsible for making the decision to do so in accordance with formally drawn up local planning policy, unless there are sound reasons for coming to a different conclusion (see Chapter 3). Therefore, planning policies are the prime consideration in whether planning permission will be given.

Remember this

Check planning policies early on to see how a project measures up.

Planning applications

Permission is needed for development; consequently there is an application process for seeking that permission. Two types of planning application can be made. First, there are 'full' or 'detailed' applications. These show all aspects of the proposal and are specific about precisely what would be built, what alterations would be made or what use would be made of land or buildings. Second, there are outline applications. These are made to establish, in principle, whether a building can be built, leaving some or all details of the scheme to be determined subsequently. Outline applications can only be made for buildings not for changes of use, including conversions. The details of the building and site layout are called 'reserved matters', because they are reserved from the outline application. Another type of application is then made for the approval of reserved matters within the scope of the original outline permission. Once they have been approved, the outline and reserved matters together are the equivalent of a full planning permission.

Although planning permission is supposed to be obtained for development before it takes place, inevitably building work and changes of use happen without the necessary consent. In these circumstances, an application can be made for permission after the event. This is generally referred to as 'retrospective' planning permission.

There are various other applications which can be made after planning permission has been granted. Conditions are attached to permissions (see Chapter 4) and there is a procedure for applying to remove or vary conditions. In certain circumstances, this type of application can be used to make changes to the design or layout of an approved scheme (see Chapter 8). There is a separate procedure for making very minor changes to a planning permission, called a non-material amendment. One condition attached to a planning permission is a time limit within which to begin the development permitted; this is usually three years for full planning permission (five years in Northern Ireland and Wales). Applications to extend the duration of planning permission are often referred to as 'renewals' although they are, technically, new applications.

Remember this
If it is not clear, ask the council which type of application is appropriate.

Other consents

Sometimes special applications have to be made either in conjunction with planning applications or separately. Buildings and structures with exceptional historical or architectural value are given special protection. They are included on a list of such buildings and, hence, are called 'listed' buildings. Most work to listed buildings needs listed building consent (see Chapter 2), in addition to any planning permission required. Conservation Areas are designated to preserve areas of distinctive character. Most demolition of structures in Conservation Areas has to have Conservation Area consent (see Chapter 2).

Circumstances may arise where it is desirable to establish whether planning permission for a particular development is necessary and/or whether the development is beyond the council's powers to prevent or undo it. In these cases a 'lawful development certificate' application can be made (see Chapter 2).

Much new building work and some changes of use require approval under the building regulations. This is a completely separate regime to planning.

Planning appeals

Of course, not all planning applications are successful and the system includes an appeals process. Appeals are made to central government bodies: the Planning Inspectorate in England and Wales, and the Planning Appeals Commission in Northern Ireland. The appeals system in Scotland is a little different. Appeals against decisions taken by council officers are decided by a group of elected councillors. Appeals against decisions taken by the council's planning committee are made to the Scottish Government's Directorate for Planning and Environmental Appeals.

Appeals can be made when a council refuses permission, fails to make a decision within set time periods, or grants planning permission subject to conditions which the applicant wishes to vary or remove.

Appeals provide the opportunity for the merits of a proposed development to be considered by an independent inspector (reporter in Scotland, commissioner in Northern Ireland), free of local politics. Appeal decisions, and the interpretations they contain, are supposed to be taken into account by councils when deciding planning applications. Thus the appeals system is intended to keep a check on councils and to provide some consistency in decisions between councils.

Key idea

The council's decision is not necessarily final.

Enforcement

While development is meant to be permitted before it goes ahead, some is undertaken without the necessary consent. This is known as a 'breach of planning control'. People are sometimes unaware of the need for permission, planning regulations are complicated and it might not be clear whether permission is required, and others are willing to take a chance. It is not against the criminal law to carry out development without planning permission, but undertaking work on listed buildings or demolishing buildings in Conservation Areas without the necessary consents are criminal offences.

Councils have various powers to stop unauthorized development, have land and buildings reinstated or buildings taken down. These powers are called 'enforcement'. Councils do not have to act just because a development did not have permission, and they are expected to weigh up whether unacceptable harm has been, or is being, caused. Councils have the power to go onto land, to investigate and to serve papers on owners and occupiers requiring them to provide information. Unauthorized development can, in some circumstances, be resolved voluntarily or by submitting a planning application or lawful development certificate application (see Chapter 2). Otherwise, the council has a range of notices it can serve, the most frequently used being an enforcement notice. This specifies what development the council believes is unauthorized, the action to be taken and a timescale for remedying the breach of control. A person who is served with an enforcement notice can comply with the terms or appeal against it, which is similar to a planning appeal. If the person does neither, the council can prosecute, which can result in fines being imposed and/or work being undertaken at the offender's expense.

Key idea

Councils have powers to take action against any development without planning permission.

Focus points

* The planning system controls development – the construction of buildings and change of use of land and buildings.
* Planning permission is required for development.
* Council and government planning policies are the starting point for deciding applications for planning permission.
* Applicants for planning permission can appeal if refused permission.

Next step

Having understood what the planning system is and what it does in a general sense, the next key points to consider are precisely what is exempt from the need for planning permission, what needs permission and, of those projects, which require a planning application to be submitted to the council.

The need for planning permission

In this chapter you will learn:

- ▶ *What development is*
- ▶ *When planning permission is required*
- ▶ *Which projects require a planning application*
- ▶ *About development without planning permission*
- ▶ *How listed buildings, Conservation Areas and protected trees affect planning permission*

The definition of development

Planning legislation says that planning permission is needed for carrying out development so anyone contemplating a project needs to know what the definition of development encompasses. The law defines development as:

- carrying out building operations;

- making a material change of use of buildings or land;

- carrying out engineering, mining or other operations.

BUILDING WORK
Building operations are further defined as including:

- demolition of buildings;

- rebuilding;

- structural alterations or additions to buildings;

- other operations normally carried out by a builder.

The definition of a building includes any structure or erection and any part of a building. Thus, the net is cast quite wide and takes in most structures from houses to extensions, garages, sheds, decking and even very minor works to buildings, such as painting. It also includes the rebuilding of a building exactly as it was before. At the lowest level, however, there are some exclusions from the definition. Maintenance, improvement or other building alterations do not need permission, provided they are either internal work or do not materially affect the external appearance of the building. This means that knocking down walls, moving a staircase or making new doorways inside a building will not need planning permission (although building regulations consent or listed building consent might be needed). Which minor external works do need permission is a matter of opinion based on the interpretation of what constitutes a 'material' change to the external appearance. For example, repainting a building the same colour as it was before would not need permission. The matter has to be judged on whether the changes would be visible from normal vantage points. Consequently, there is more latitude in places that cannot be seen from outside the site. While many alterations to houses require planning permission, they do not actually necessitate a planning application for the reason explained below.

Key idea

Work inside a building does not need planning permission.

On the face of it, what constitutes a building might seem quite straightforward. In practice there are grey areas. For example, a marquee put up for a short period is not usually regarded as the same as erecting a building, but if it is left up permanently, or for prolonged periods, it could be considered to constitute a building. Stationing a caravan is a use of land rather than a building operation but when it is bricked-up underneath, a porch and some decking is attached and so on, a point can be reached where it becomes a building. Movable field shelters for horses have been deemed items merely resting on the land in some instances and buildings in others. Court decisions have established three tests – size, permanence and physical attachment to the ground – to help ascertain whether a structure is a building for planning purposes.

CHANGE OF USE

Change of use refers to more obvious changes such as a flat becoming an office, part of an agricultural field being annexed to a domestic garden or a barn being converted into a house. However, there are many areas where the concept is not clear cut, partly because the definition applies only to 'material' changes of use, so a change of use is not enough on its own but has to be considered to be material. In other words, the change has to be discernible and have consequences, such as appearance, noise or activity. Some changes are specifically excluded from the need for planning permission, including using land or buildings in the curtilage (garden) of a house for any incidental residential purpose, such as a games room, car parking, recreation and domestic storage. In an effort to simplify change of use planning permission, the government categorizes uses into various classes and the law says that changes between uses, within a defined class, will not need planning permission. Some uses are specifically excluded from the defined classes and these are called *sui generis* uses. The various use classes are:

- A1 Shops

- A2 Financial and professional services

- A3 Restaurants and cafes

- A4 Drinking establishments

- A5 Hot food takeaways

- B1 Business

- B2 General industrial

- B8 Storage or distribution

- C1 Hotels

- C2 Residential institutions

- C2a Secure residential institutions

- C3 Dwelling-houses

- C4 Houses in multiple occupation

- D1 Non-residential institutions

- D2 Assembly and leisure

So, for example, a high street shop changing from a hairdresser's or travel agency to a dry cleaner's or undertaker's will not need planning permission because all of these businesses fall within the shops use class. The dwelling-house class includes family use, up to six people living as one household and up to six people living as one household and receiving care. Switching between these types of occupation is not, therefore, development. However, for the reason explained below, in the section on permitted development, not all material changes of use require a planning application to be made, even though they are considered to be development.

The scope of material change of use is wide enough to allow ancillary or incidental uses as part of the overall use of a property, providing they are related and subsidiary to the main use and do not have significant consequences. For example, a room used by a householder for low-key office use to run a business will not need planning permission. On the other hand, a householder letting out a garden outbuilding to someone else for running a business would be likely to require permission because the link with the occupiers of the house would be broken.

In many cases, building work is part and parcel of a change of use, for example, where a farm building is converted to a dwelling. In these circumstances one planning permission for the conversion wraps up both the building works and the change of use.

ENGINEERING OPERATIONS

There is no definition of engineering operations beyond the legislation stating that it includes forming an access, and case law determining that it includes operations generally supervised by an engineer, whether or not an engineer is actually employed. In practice, engineering operations are works such as excavation, creating or removing embankments and laying surfacing or hard standings, as well as constructing an access. Engineering operations, for example digging foundations, are often part and parcel of construction projects but separate permission is not necessary for those elements.

Key idea

Most building work and changes of use need planning permission.

Permitted development

The definition of development requiring planning permission is wide, and if every small-scale project necessitated a planning application to the council, the planning system would be over burdened. To avoid this, planning law allows central government to grant blanket planning permission for various categories of development which are set out in a government order. This type of permission is called 'permitted development'. There are different regulations in each country of the UK. Projects within the scope of the defined classes of permitted development in the order can, in most cases, just go straight ahead. A few types of permitted development project have to be notified to the council in advance and the council can then exercise some limited control over the proposal. These include changing the use of offices to residential, demolition and some large rear extensions.

In England and Wales, there are over 40 categories of permitted development with various classes within each category. These relate to development on houses, minor works including domestic micro-generation equipment, changes of use, caravans, agricultural buildings, CCTV, commercial developments, and a range of other works undertaken by public bodies, crown properties, telecommunication companies and so on. Various changes are allowed between the types of use defined in the government's use classes order (see above). So, for example, a pub can switch to being a shop or industrial buildings can be used for light industry or offices.

The main types of permitted development relevant to residential properties (in England) are shown in Table 2.1. Householder rights do not apply to flats, maisonettes, mixed-use properties or houses in multiple occupation. The rights are more restricted in Conservation Areas, Areas of Outstanding Natural Beauty (AONBs) and National Parks. Some rights do not apply to listed properties but, in any event, permitted development rights do not override the need to obtain listed building consent.

Table 2.1 Domestic permitted development rights

Householder	Any residential property
Extensions, improvements and alterations to houses	Gates, fences and walls
Roof extensions	Means of access
Other roof alterations	Painting the exterior of any building
Porches	Demolition
Outbuildings, swimming pools, enclosures and domestic heating fuel containers	Change of use to and from a small house in multiple occupation (up to six people)
Hard surfacing	Change of use from offices (excluding certain defined locations)
Chimneys, flues or soil and vent pipes	
Microwave antennas	

The concept of permitted development is simple; the reality is more complicated. Each class has limits and criteria to meet; applying the regulations involves interpretation and different councils have different views on some aspects. The right to carry out development on and around houses applies only to the curtilage. In most cases this equates to the garden but for houses with large grounds, or with paddocks or orchards or where adjoining land in non-residential use has been annexed, the extent of curtilage might not be so clear.

Key idea

Many domestic projects are given permission automatically by a government order.

Councils have the power to take away specified permitted development rights in defined areas, typically in Conservation Areas. Also, in many residential areas where there is a high concentration of students, the right that would otherwise be available to owners to change houses into small houses in multiple occupation, has been removed. The means to do this is called an Article 4 Direction. Councils usually publicize the existence of Article 4 Directions and keep public records of where directions are in force. When granting planning permission, councils can put a condition on the permission taking away permitted development rights. This might be done, for example, on a conversion where the council wants to retain the character of the original building, on a constrained site where further building could result in over-development or to maintain privacy of a neighbouring property by preventing new window openings on certain elevations of the building. Where permitted development is restricted by these means, it does not mean the development cannot ever be carried out, just that a planning application would have to be made to seek permission for it.

Information and guidance about the detail and application of permitted development is available on the websites of the UK governments: for England and Wales (www.planningportal.gov.uk); for Scotland (www.scotland.gov.uk/Topics/built-environment/planning); and for Northern Ireland (www.planningni.gov.uk).

Since the right to undertake permitted development is fraught with uncertainties, there is a way to establish whether the proposed work or use is within the permitted development regulations. This is explained later in this chapter.

NEIGHBOURHOOD DEVELOPMENT ORDERS

Since 2012, town or parish councils and community groups in England have had the power to put in place, what are in practice, local permitted development rights in a neighbourhood development order. The rights apply only in the defined neighbourhood area and each order specifies what types of development can take place without the need to apply to the council for planning permission in the usual way. Information about any orders in force should be on the district council's website.

Projects that require a planning application

Taking into account the definition of development requiring planning permission and planning permission given by permitted development order, the most common projects relating to houses that do and do not typically require a planning application to the council are set out in Table 2.2. Other consents might still be needed (see below). This is only a general guide and it is advisable to check with the council or with a professional before spending time or money on a project.

There are some areas where the need for planning permission is open to interpretation and councils and planning inspectors adopt varying approaches. Where there is doubt, councils often err on the side of caution.

ANNEXES

A residential annexe, occupied by members of the household, which could be family or domestic staff, does not necessarily require planning permission. This can be the case even when the annexe is physically separate from the main house and possesses all facilities necessary for independent living, such as a kitchen and bathroom. However, the greater the connection between

Table 2.2

Needs planning application	Does not need a planning application
Building a new house, including replacing an existing house	Internal alterations
Adding a storey to an existing house	Repairs, maintenance and like-for-like replacements of building elements
Raising the roof of an existing house	Extensions to houses*
Subdividing a house or flat into two houses or flats	Porches*
Garages in front of houses*	New doors and windows*
Converting non-residential buildings (other than most offices in England) to houses	Replacement double glazing*
Using a house or outbuilding for non-residential use (except for small houses in multiple occupation*)	Painting and repainting*
	Solar and photovoltaic panels*
	Working from home (providing it is low impact)
Some large extensions*	Having a lodger or using a room for B&B
Side and two-storey rear extensions in Conservation Areas, AONBs or National Parks	Using garden buildings for residential purposes
Most front extensions*	Garden buildings*
Raised decking*	Swimming pools*
Balconies and verandas	Tennis courts*
External cladding in Conservation Areas, AONBs or National Parks*	Laying paths, patios, paving and hard standings*
Incorporating non-residential land into a garden	Creating accesses onto unclassified roads*
Creating an access onto a classified road*	* where the project is within the scope of permitted development rights
Development prohibited by a condition on a planning permission	
* where the project is outside the scope of permitted development	

the occupation of the annexe and the house, the less likely it is that permission is required. The two buildings being physically attached, having interconnecting doors, the annexe being reliant on the house for some facilities, for example laundry or cooking, frequent to-ing and fro-ing, perhaps for care or baby-sitting purposes and shared access and parking, all increase the likelihood that permission is unnecessary.

When constructing an annexe attached to a house, the building itself could come within permitted development rights for extensions. Where a separate building is built as a permitted development, a quirk of the system dictates that it cannot be first occupied as living accommodation. Consequently, permitted development rights cannot be used to build an annexe. However, as long as an existing outbuilding remains within the same planning unit as the house, using it for residential accommodation by members of the household should not be considered to be a material change of use. So, an existing building can, potentially, be used as an annexe. There is no set time period for a permitted development garden building to become considered an existing building but it would have to have a genuine non-living accommodation use first.

CARAVANS

Similar considerations apply to stationing a caravan or mobile home in a garden for use by members of the household. Stationing a caravan is a use rather than a building because a caravan just rests on the ground and is considered to be a transient thing. Consequently, permitted development is not involved along with the associated new building/existing building issue. There is no definition of a caravan in planning legislation and the definition from the Caravan Sites Act is generally adopted. That definition includes certain maximum dimensions, and construction and movability criteria. A mobile home can be a caravan for planning purposes.

Subject to coming under the definition of a caravan, the considerations regarding occupation are the same as for an annexe. By definition, a caravan is designed for human habitation and most caravans are equipped for self-contained occupation. Obviously, a caravan cannot be attached to a house but proximity to it could influence the decision on whether it requires permission. The caravan would have to be stationed within the planning unit of the house, which is most likely to coincide with the garden. Locating it within an adjoining field, for example, would put it outside the planning unit, even if the field was in the same ownership, and permission would be needed. If a caravan occupied by a member of the household were judged not to be part and parcel of the use of the residential property, planning permission would be required for its occupation as an independent unit. Parking a touring caravan in a garden or on a drive does not normally need planning permission.

RUNNING A BUSINESS FROM HOME

A householder does not necessarily need planning permission to run a business or work from home. At one end of the spectrum is using a kitchen table or spare room as an office. At the other end could be several rooms or outbuildings being used, noisy machinery, staff, materials and equipment being stored and a constant stream of visitors. It is easy to see that the absence of impact with the former would not trigger a need for planning permission but the latter would clearly be material. In between the two extremes is a grey area. As with all such questions, the decision on whether the use should have permission is for the council initially and a planning inspector on appeal, thereafter.

The main test is whether the character of the use of the property would change as a result of the business activity. Criteria applied include the proportion of the property used for the business, the number of staff and visitors, the amount of traffic generated, whether goods would be stored outside and the noise levels. Activities such as office use, childminding, tutoring, hairdressing, repairing computers, dressmaking, medical treatment or therapy could all potentially be carried out at home with having any detrimental impact on neighbours or even being noticeable.

MULTIPLE OCCUPANCY

Normal residential use for planning purposes is occupation by a household in which occupiers cook, eat and socialize together, and share the facilities of the house. The occupants do not, however, have to be relatives. Occupation by people who have no prior connection and do not live together as one household is considered to be multiple occupancy, which is a change of use. That is not to say that such a change of use is necessarily a material change. Whether people are living as a household or leading separate lives, albeit sharing some or all facilities, such as bathrooms and kitchens, can be a fine judgement. Points used to test the matter can include whether occupants have individual rental agreements, whether they know each other before moving in, whether bedrooms are locked, whether occupants share food and cook and eat together and whether there are communal rooms where they spend time together. Also taken into account is whether there are any external consequences of multiple occupation which would distinguish it from single household use.

Some of the difficulties of interpretation were avoided in England by the introduction of a permitted development right to change between ordinary single dwelling use and small houses in multiple occupation. The right allows for occupation by up to six people. Whether a seventh person would automatically trigger a material change of use is debatable. The permitted development right can be withdrawn by councils. In locations where this has been done, questions remain over whether occupiers are living as one household.

Remember this

Check the need for an application with the council before undertaking significant projects.

Lawful development

As set out in preceding sections, there are many instances where it is not clear whether planning permission is required. Also, where a project is going to rely on permitted development rights, it is often desirable to have the certainty that the council agrees the proposal does, indeed, come within the scope of the regulations. Prospective purchasers of properties (or their solicitors) often want reassurance that work or a use was duly authorized. Questions about the need for planning permission can arise after work has taken place or a change of use is made. The planning system provides a means to establish whether a proposed development or an existing development is lawful, that is, whether it would be or is within planning law and regulations.

To establish lawfulness, another type of application is made to the council, similar to a planning application in some respects but serving a different purpose. This is an application for a lawful development certificate. These applications can be made on the basis of a proposed project or an existing one. If the council is satisfied that the project would be or is lawful, it will issue a certificate to formally confirm that. In considering such applications, the council is supposed to assess only whether the project is within the law, not whether it believes it is desirable, as it would for a planning application. A lawful development certificate should be a purely legal determination. Unlike planning permission, conditions cannot be put on these certificates.

Development without planning permission

As noted in Chapter 1, projects sometimes take place without the required planning permission. Planning law provides that, after certain periods of time have elapsed, unauthorized work or use becomes lawful. For building work and other operations, the period is four years from completion of the work. In the case of using a building as a single dwelling-house, the period is four years from when the use began. For all other types of development, including not complying with a planning condition on a previously granted planning permission, the period of time is ten years from when the breach of planning control first occurred. If the unauthorized project is in breach of an enforcement notice, the development does not become lawful after any time. Where a council can show there has been deliberate concealment of the development, it can take enforcement action beyond the standard time periods.

Building work is relatively easy to establish, although there can be uncertainty over when the work is deemed to have been completed. Uses are often much more complicated. To qualify, uses must be consistent throughout the period. In the case of using a building as a residence, the building must be considered to be a dwelling-house, which can rule out some structures not readily recognisable as a house. If the residential use is part of a mixed use, the time limit is ten years rather than four. Living in a mobile home on land is a use, not a building, so is subject to the ten-year rule. Where a property is used in breach of a planning condition, any significant gaps in that use will reset the clock and the ten years start again.

Once the relevant time period has passed, the owner can apply for a lawful development certificate to establish that the development is now lawful and, therefore, beyond the council's powers to take action against it. Evidence has to be submitted with the application to prove what has taken place and when, in order to obtain a certificate.

Key idea

After certain time periods have elapsed, councils can no longer take action against unauthorized building work and uses.

Listed buildings

Once a building is listed as having special architectural or historical interest, additional protection applies, beyond normal planning control which continues to apply. Any work for demolition, alteration or extension, which would affect a listed building's character, requires listed building consent. Applications for this consent are very similar to planning applications and are also made to the council, with similar rights of appeal. The definition of development for planning permission purposes does not apply to listed building consent and permitted development rights do not affect the need to obtain listed building consent. This means many minor works, such as painting a listed building or part of it a different colour, and work to the interior of the building can require listed building consent. There is no equivalent of lawful development certificates for listed building work. Consequently, any work which might conceivably affect the character of the building is best discussed with the council to get clearance for it. Undertaking work that affects character without the necessary listed building consent is a criminal offence.

Conservation Areas

Conservation Areas are designated by councils for their special architectural or historical interest, and this means their character and/or appearance should preserved or enhanced. Once an area is designated, there are several additional restrictions affecting development and the need for planning permission. Demolition of buildings in Conservation Areas requires Conservation Area consent, independent of the need for planning permission. These applications are similar to planning applications and are usually made at the same time where both are necessary. Small buildings and gates, walls and fences below certain heights are excluded from the need for Conservation Area consent, as are listed buildings, because they are already covered by listed building protection.

Permitted development rights are more limited in Conservation Areas. This includes no rights for side extensions or two-storey rear extensions, external cladding, dormer windows and garden buildings to the side of the house.

All trees with a diameter of 75 mm or more, measuring 1.5 m above ground level, in Conservation Areas are protected and any work on such trees should not take place without first serving a notice on the council. Work on trees that are dead, dying or dangerous are exempt, although even here it is as well to check with the council that it agrees with the diagnosis. The council has six weeks within which to issue a tree preservation order (see below) or to indicate the work can go ahead and, if it does neither, the work can proceed.

Tree preservation orders

Councils have the power to protect trees where they feel that would be 'expedient in the interests of amenity'. This is done by issuing a tree preservation order (TPO). These can be applied to individual trees, groups of trees, an area or woodlands. Protection does not extend to dead, dying or dangerous trees or to commercially cultivated fruit trees where the work is in the interests of the business. Once protected, trees cannot be felled, pruned or damaged, including cutting roots, without the council's consent. Trees can be felled without consent in order to implement a planning permission given by the council. Applications have to be made in writing, specifying and giving reasons for the work proposed. Councils provide application forms which can be used for this purpose. The council can then decide whether or not to grant consent, with or without conditions.

Hedgerows also enjoy protection in England and Wales. It is against the law to remove most countryside hedgerows without permission. Hedgerows bordering houses are exempted. As with TPOs, applications to remove hedgerows are made to the council which can refuse or allow the application. Note that for both protected trees and hedgerows, removal without permission is a criminal offence.

Remember this

Check whether trees are protected before carrying out work or felling them.

Focus points

* Planning permission is required for buildings and material changes of use.
* The government gives planning permission for certain types of development in a permitted development order so an application does not have to be made.
* Larger-scale projects require a planning application to be submitted.
* The lawfulness of development can be tested by a lawful development certificate application.
* Additional permissions can be required in the case of listed buildings, Conservation Areas and protected trees.

Next step

Having established what projects are likely to
necessitate a planning application to the council,
the next issue that arises is the basis on which
applications are supposed to be decided and what
factors are relevant to the consideration of a
proposed development.

The basis for making planning decisions

In this chapter you will learn:

▶ *How planning policies form the basis of planning decisions*

▶ *About neighbourhood and local plans, and how to get involved in shaping them*

▶ *What guidance is available*

▶ *About 'material considerations'*

Legal basis for determining planning applications

The legal basis for deciding planning applications is contained in one deceptively simple sentence of planning law. This says that planning decisions should be made in accordance with the policies of the development plan, unless 'material considerations' indicate otherwise. Councils or inspectors considering planning applications or appeals should use this as the basis for their decisions.

Planning policies set out in development plans are frequently under review, so it is by no means always clear what actually constitutes the 'development plan'. Similarly, precisely which considerations are material and how much weight to put on them are often points of debate in decision making. Fortunately, the many levels of previous planning policies have been slimmed down. Where the development plan once comprised regional plans, county structure plans and district local plans, now there is only the district plan and, in some areas, specific neighbourhood plans to contend with. That slimming down was part of a general move towards less 'top down' planning, and greater emphasis on individual communities.

A key material consideration is government planning policy guidance with which local policies are supposed to fall in line. Government policy is set out in policy statements, circulars, ministerial pronouncements and a variety of additional guidelines relevant to decisions. Finally, the basis for decision making is constantly being refined through appeal and court decisions, adding an additional layer of case law and precedent to the mix.

To unravel the basis for decision making, the following sections look at the different layers of planning policy and at which material considerations should and should not be taken into account in planning decisions.

Key idea

Planning decisions should be made in accordance with the policies of the development plan, unless 'material considerations' indicate otherwise.

Neighbourhood plans

Neighbourhood plans were brought into being in England in 2012. They enable individual communities to help shape what gets built where and when. Unlike other layers of planning policy, neighbourhood plans are optional; it is for communities to decide whether they want a neighbourhood plan. In part, that might depend on there being individuals or groups within the community who are willing and able to take on the challenge of preparing a plan and agreeing its contents with the sometimes competing interests within the community. Neighbourhoods cannot use their plans to block developments proposed or approved by the district council. Neighbourhood plans must be in line with local and national planning policies and with planning law. While they cannot be used to resist development, they can influence the types of homes and commercial buildings built, together with details such as design and location.

Communities are represented by a neighbourhood forum which takes on the task of preparing the neighbourhood plan. That forum would normally be the parish or town council but does not have to be, if there is no such council representing the area. Once the neighbourhood forum has produced a draft plan, it is considered by an independent examiner to ensure it meets all the guidelines. After a successful examination, the district council organizes a local referendum where the plan needs at least a 50 per cent vote in favour. If this is achieved, the plan is then formally adopted by the district council and acquires legal force as part of the development plan for the area.

Communities can also grant planning permission for developments in line with the neighbourhood plan, via neighbourhood development orders (see Chapter 2).

Key idea

Neighbourhoods can greatly influence planning decisions through neighbourhood plans.

Local plans

Local plans are the key policy documents used by councils in determining planning applications. The equivalents in Scotland and Wales are local development plans and, in Northern Ireland, development plans. In England, local plans were formerly called 'local development frameworks' and so some documents might still bear that name. Policies in some even older documents have been 'saved' for the time being and these might still be in use too.

The local plans system has undergone change in recent years and councils often have a range of planning policy documents as a result of this transition. To find out which policies apply to applications in an area, speak to a planning officer in the council's planning policy section. Information about policy on council websites is often very comprehensive but does not necessarily make clear which of the draft, adopted and emerging policies are actually in use at any moment.

Remember this

Get confirmation of which policy documents are current from council planning policy officers.

Local plans consist of a written document or documents, comprising polices and explanatory text, and maps, known as 'proposal maps'. Where there is more than one written document, typically, they comprise: a core strategy, setting out broad principles; a development control policy document, providing the detailed policies for different types of buildings and uses; and a development sites document, setting out where new buildings and estates are proposed to be built. The maps show where the different policies apply within the council's area. The main proposals map shows the whole of the district. Larger-scale plans, known as 'inset maps', show details of areas like town centres and individual settlements. Some councils also have online mapping systems enabling users to focus on particular locations, where the policies that apply to them are revealed. Others have inset maps as separate documents that can be viewed alongside a key to the colours and lines which indicate policy areas.

LOCAL PLAN POLICIES

Local plan policies cover a wide range of topics. Typically these include:

- general strategy
- general development control criteria
- Green Belt (in districts with Green Belt areas)
- design
- sustainability
- heritage
- countryside
- housing
- employment
- tourism and leisure
- transport
- community
- issues specific to an area

Different councils use different language and grouping of policies. For example, design and general development control policies are sometimes run together. Policies concerning replacement dwellings and house extensions in the countryside might be found under a housing heading or could be under countryside. Tourism could pop up under employment but there could also be policies under countryside. The following sections look at common local plan chapters and the sort of policies they typically contain.

General strategy

These policies set the tone for other more specific policies within the plan. They can be aspirational, seeking to foster a sense of community and good health and welfare. They can also be locational, directing development to specific locations, such as utilizing brownfield (previously developed) sites in favour of greenfield (undeveloped), or focusing new building within prescribed built-up areas. Emphasis is likely to be put on ensuring all new development meets sustainability criteria.

▶ General development control criteria

All applications must follow the basic rules of good planning and these are found in varying degrees of detail in these general policies. They include:

▶ protecting the amenities of neighbours, such as privacy, peace and quiet, and outlook;

▶ accounting for the future needs of occupiers, including disabled access;

▶ providing adequate and safe access and parking and avoiding traffic congestion;

▶ respecting the character and appearance of the street and wider area;

▶ preserving heritage assets, such as listed buildings and Conservation Areas;

▶ conserving landscape and natural beauty;

▶ protecting habitats of ecological value;

▶ deterring crime;

▶ promoting efficient use of energy;

▶ providing adequate drainage;

▶ ensuring adequate infrastructure and facilities are available;

▶ avoiding flood risk;

▶ preventing the loss of high quality agricultural land;

▶ addressing known or suspected contamination.

Many of these general policy criteria will be elaborated on elsewhere in the plan.

▶ Green Belt

In districts with designated Green Belt, there are always specific policies to ensure the protection and permanence of the designated area. Green Belts are defined around major urban areas to prevent them extending ever outwards and merging with neighbouring towns and villages. Policies prohibit most types of new building, including housing, in Green Belt, although limited extension and rebuilding is permitted, in addition to limited infilling within some settlements.

▶ Design

Design policies can be general, encouraging a high standard of design in all developments. They can also be specific, referring to particular areas where design might play a role in enhancing local character. Some design policies are supportive of innovation while others place greater emphasis on preserving local building styles. Policies can also cover the internal arrangement of accommodation, especially for residential buildings which can be required to meet existing and changing needs of diverse households.

▶ Sustainability

These policies might relate to the energy efficiency of new buildings, use of renewable energy technology, location of development, recycling and minimizing waste. Residential buildings can be required to meet certain performance standards to minimize use of resources and fossil fuels in construction and use.

▶ Heritage

Heritage policies address development in Conservation Areas, and works to or affecting listed buildings. They also define any of the council's own non-statutory heritage designations, such as 'areas of townscape value', 'locally listed' buildings and so on, and set out criteria that apply to development covered by these designations.

Countryside

Policies can be either general or specific and apply to different forms of development. General policies establish how countryside is to be protected and where such policies apply. They also concern development in specially designated areas, such as Areas of Outstanding Natural Beauty (National Scenic Areas in Scotland) and any local landscape protection designations. More specific topics covered might include ecological protection, agricultural development and diversification and housing, business and tourism proposals in the countryside.

Housing

Housing policies fall into two distinct camps. The first is concerned with how much housing should be provided and where it should be built; the second deals with the general development control and design issues applicable to new houses, replacements and extensions. The latter group can be covered by separate policies for developments in built-up areas and countryside. Detailed policies cover affordable housing and the circumstances in which it must be provided. In regard to changes to individual dwellings, specific policies can cover matters like annexes, garages and other outbuildings and the extension of gardens in the countryside.

Employment

These policies are concerned with the amount and location of new business space required, preservation of existing business space and detailed policies relating to changes of use. Different policies cover industrial, office and retail uses. The latter include town centre policies and often contain a 'shopping hierarchy' of primary, secondary and neighbourhood shopping areas, each with attendant policies.

Tourism and leisure

Leisure-related policies deal with the retention and provision of parks, sports fields and play areas as well as indoor leisure facilities. Tourism policies vary greatly depending on the nature of tourism in the particular area. For example, a seaside borough might have very detailed policies concerning hotels, whereas a rural district might have policies concerned with holiday cottages and caravan and campsites.

▶ Transport

Transport policies generally seek to promote so-called non-car modes of transport, in other words, walking, cycling and public transport. They also deal with highway safety, including new accesses onto the public highway and roads within new large-scale developments, and parking. There might also be policies for proposed new road schemes, such as bypasses.

▶ Community

These policies cover things like protection of open spaces, sport and recreation facilities, as well as other community facilities such as schools, libraries and community centres. The emphasis is generally on preservation of such facilities. Development needs infrastructure and community facilities, and there is usually a requirement to contribute funding towards those needs. Local plan policies set out the council's approach to securing that funding.

▶ Issues specific to an area

Some areas have particular industries or attributes to which specific policies apply which are not generally found elsewhere. For example, near racecourses there can be policies specific to the horse racing industry; seaside resorts could have detailed policies relating to hotels and guest houses; and National Parks are likely to have policies relating to public access and tourism.

LOCAL PLAN ADOPTION PROCESS

Local plans go through a number of distinct stages before being formally adopted by the council. The process is broadly similar throughout the UK. In England the stages are:

▶ information gathering;

▶ publication of a draft plan with an opportunity for public comment;

- consideration of comments;
- publication of a 'submission draft' plan for public comment;
- assessment by an independent inspector, including public examination;
- modification and adoption.

There are several opportunities within this process for public involvement, whether that is to promote or object to particular policies or specific development proposals. These are the points at which members of the public can make their views known in order to try to influence emerging policy and, ultimately, individual planning decisions based on those polices. Where a council's local plan is being reviewed, monitor its website carefully to discover opportunities to contribute to the process. If in doubt, call or email the council's planning policy team to find out about public consultation and likely timing.

Remember this

Help shape policy by getting involved in the local plan review process.

Supplementary guidance

Many councils produce additional planning documents, called supplementary planning documents or guidance (SPD or SPGs) which flesh out some detailed aspects of policy. The degree of consistency between supplementary guidance and adopted local plan policy, together with the amount of public consultation on such guidance, determines how much weight should be attached to it in making planning application decisions. That said, it is likely the detailed guidance in SPD/SPGs is going to be applied by the council in decision making, regardless of consistency and consultation.

SPD/SPGs can cover any aspect of policy, but frequently address matters like the provision of affordable housing, financial contributions, design guidelines and development advice specific to a particular area identified for growth or renewal.

Key idea

Councils can flesh-out local plan policies with supplementary guidance.

Government guidance

In England, the National Planning Policy Framework (NPPF) is the principal government policy document setting out the broad framework on which councils' planning policies and decisions should be based. Similar policy documents exist elsewhere: in Scotland, the National Planning Framework; in Wales, Planning Policy Wales; and in Northern Ireland there remain a number of Planning Policy Statements.

National policy guidance gives broad-brush advice to councils on how they should draw up their policies and how they should apply them when it comes to determining planning applications. The guidance covers issues like economic development, housing, design and transport, together with the natural and historic environment, infrastructure and minerals. Importantly, the guidance establishes priorities. The NPPF, for example, sets out a presumption in favour of sustainable development, a key principle supposed to underpin all planning decisions.

Councils generally place much greater weight on their own policies than on national guidance when making decisions. At appeal, though, inspectors focus on both aspects of policy. So, when you are promoting or objecting to a planning proposal, look at the relevant local plan policy and the national policy, and frame representations in light of both.

As well as the main statements of planning policy guidance in England, Scotland and Wales, there is a variety of additional guidance in the form of government circulars, advice notes and explanatory leaflets. Some of these are on technical planning subjects, such as the circulars relating to conditions on planning applications and the circumstances in which costs are awarded at appeals. Some are about certain types of development, for example business or caravan sites. Others concern development standards, such as *Manual for Streets*, which sets out specifications for road and junction layouts and design, vehicle stopping distances and parking.

Key idea
Local plan policies must be in line with government planning policy guidance.

Material considerations

As noted previously, planning decisions have to be made in accordance with the development plan, unless material considerations indicate otherwise. What exactly constitutes a material consideration is not defined in law, but in practice almost anything which relates to the use and development of land is capable of being a material consideration. Most of these factors are embodied in local and national planning policies, although national policies and ministerial guidance are themselves material considerations as they do not form part of the development plan.

Material considerations include all the things to think about when assessing a planning project, although not every material consideration applies to every project. The following are the most commonly encountered material considerations.

SUSTAINABILITY
Sustainability has been defined as meeting the needs of the present without compromising the ability of future generations to meet their own needs. In England, the NPPF defines three aspects to sustainable development: economic, social and environmental. An important part of sustainability is locating new development so as to minimize the need to travel by car. Other, more specific material considerations can be viewed in the context of sustainability to determine whether a particular project would be sustainable.

▶ Layout
The height, size and shape of any new building needs to fit physically onto the site, as well as respecting the wider pattern

of building and the character of the area. The amount of space around a building is important, as is where the building sits relative to its boundaries. Respecting building lines – the common distance from buildings to the adjoining road – can be a defining characteristic of an area and so be important in some locations. This does not mean that every new building must slavishly follow the prevailing pattern and character of the area but it does mean these things need to be considered.

▶ Design

The design of new buildings or extensions is a key material consideration. Design includes the dimensions, proportions, shape, style, materials and finishes of the building. In short, what it looks like. Whether a design is acceptable or appropriate inevitably leads into subjective judgements and matters of taste. Generally, a design needs to fit in with its surroundings, either by following adjoining designs, reflecting elements of them or perhaps by providing a contrast to them.

▶ Residential amenities

All new development is expected to respect the amenities of neighbours. It should not unacceptably reduce their privacy, outlook or garden space, nor should it block their natural light or cause noise nuisance to an excessive degree. Maintaining privacy means avoiding overlooking the windows of habitable rooms, namely living, dining, kitchen and bedrooms. The same goes for private gardens, with patios and outdoor seating areas close to the house being the most sensitive to overlooking. Outlook must be distinguished from a view. Where one or more window looks out into some space, building something in front of it, i.e. removing that outlook, can be considered unacceptable. Similarly, reducing the amount of daylight reaching habitable rooms is a material planning consideration (and also potentially an infringement of a resident's legal right to light). Tall or bulky development close to boundaries can be inappropriately overbearing for adjoining residents.

Noise from new access drives and parking areas can be an issue where they adjoin existing houses and gardens. Industrial processes, social activities, including pubs and restaurants, plant and machinery, including extract systems from commercial kitchens and heating or air conditioning systems can all potentially cause noise nuisance. Noise, and amenities generally, are judged against prevailing levels. A new noise source in an inner city environment may scarcely register above background levels but be quite intrusive in a quiet rural location.

▶ Access and parking

Most new development requires access for vehicles. The principal access considerations are highway safety, physical adequacy of the access and the provision of parking and turning space.

A new access, or an increase in the use of an existing one, is expected to be safe. Emerging vehicles should have good visibility of traffic approaching from each direction and such traffic must be able to see emerging vehicles. Bends in the road, hills, street furniture and buildings, fences, hedges and trees can all restrict visibility. The faster the speed of traffic in the road, the greater the visibility needs to be.

Vehicles should be able to enter and leave a property forwards, the exception being quiet estate roads and cul de sacs, where reversing out is acceptable. This means having adequate space on site for a vehicle to turn around. An access serving several new houses or larger commercial development might need a double width access to prevent traffic stopping in the road when a vehicle is exiting the site, as well as turning for service vehicles.

Parking requirements vary from council to council which set standards for different types of development. The need for off-road parking can be reduced or eliminated in situations where there is plentiful public or on-road car parking available or there is good access to public transport.

▶ Environment

Potential harmful impacts on trees, hedges, plants and animals, especially protected species, are all material considerations, as are the positive effects of landscaping and other measures intended to enhance the natural environment. Extra weight is attached to preserving trees and hedgerows which enjoy statutory protection. Areas of particular ecological value and rare habitats may be afforded statutory protection if designated a Site of Special Scientific Interest (SSSI), and European laws control areas given Special Protection Area (SPA) status. The latter are capable of influencing development, not just within the designated area, but for some distance around it. Land that has had a past use involving industrial processes or chemicals can be contaminated. The risk to subsequent residential occupiers is considered in planning decisions.

▶ Physical factors

There are many physical factors that can influence how or where development takes place. The presence of buildings or other obstacles on a site, its topography, underlying ground conditions, and availability and location of services are common constraints which might dictate the position of a building on a site. Physical constraints are unlikely to trump other considerations, such as fitting in with the pattern of development in the area or preserving a neighbour's amenities.

▶ Special designations

Historic buildings and parks can be subject to 'listing' – included on a statutory list – whereby they are afforded protection by law. In decision making, significant weight is attached to preserving the special interest of properties subject to such designations as well as their settings. In some cases, development that would not normally be allowed, such as housing in the countryside, might be accepted if it directly enabled the preservation of a listed structure. This is known as 'enabling development'.

Built-up areas of special historic character can be designated as Conservation Areas where, again, there is statutory protection. The effect of development on the character and appearance of Conservation Areas are important material considerations. Buildings, the spaces between them, and views and vistas within a Conservation Area can all contribute to character and so be features to be preserved.

In the countryside, attractive landscapes may be designated as an Area of Outstanding Natural Beauty (National Scenic Areas in Scotland) or as a National Park. Both designations carry high levels of protection of the quality of the landscape.

▶ Green Belt

The designation of land around cities as Green Belt is a long established part of planning law and practice. Most new building is deemed to be inappropriate in Green Belt and the restrictions are applied very strictly. So-called 'very special circumstances' have to exist to justify development defined as inappropriate. A limited group of types of development not considered to be inappropriate is set out in the NPPF:

- ▶ Buildings for agriculture and forestry.

- ▶ Facilities for outdoor sport, outdoor recreation and for cemeteries, provided openness and Green Belt purposes are not affected.

- ▶ Extension or alteration of a building, provided it does not result in disproportionate additions over and above the size of the original building.

- ▶ Replacement of a building, provided the new building is in the same use and not materially larger than the one it replaces.

- ▶ Limited infilling in villages and limited affordable housing for local community needs under policies set out in the Local Plan.

- ▶ Limited infilling or the partial or complete re-development of previously developed sites (brownfield land), whether redundant or in continuing use (excluding temporary buildings), provided openness and Green Belt purposes are not affected.

▶ Flood risk

It is generally undesirable for vulnerable uses, including residential, to be sited in locations liable to flooding. However, in some places, entire areas are subject to flood risk and there might not be an alternative. The main sources of flooding are the sea and rivers. Flood maps are published by the Environment Agency, Scottish Environment Protection Agency, or Rivers Agency in Northern Ireland, and areas at risk of flooding are often shown in local plan proposals maps. Unless there are no sites outside the flood-risk zone, proposals for vulnerable development in such zones are unlikely to be permitted.

▶ Archaeology

Areas containing archaeological remains can be subject to local or national designation. The latter designates sites of particular archaeological value and interest as Scheduled Ancient Monuments, where there is a strong presumption against development that might cause harm. The potential for archaeological remains does not necessarily prevent planning permission being given. Developers are normally required either to excavate a site and record what is found or to employ an archaeologist to watch over the works, in particular the digging of foundations.

▶ Planning history

The planning history of a site is the record of past applications, refusals, permissions and appeals. If, for example, there was a past planning permission on a site that could still be implemented, then that would be an important material consideration against which any alternative scheme would have to be judged. Similarly, comments found in appeal inspectors' decision letters should be taken into account in future planning decisions on the same site. Applicants and councils risk having costs awarded against them at appeal were an inspector's opinion to be ignored. What is said in the course of deciding previous applications does not bind a council or inspector when subsequent applications are made. However, previous statements, conclusions and decisions can be influential.

▶ Precedent

Every planning decision has to be taken on its merits. At the same time, councils should apply their policies consistently and fairly.

It is reasonable, therefore, to say that precedent can be a valid planning argument but also that it needs to be used carefully. For example, planning policy is constantly shifting, so decisions taken even in the recent past might not have been based on exactly the same policies as now. Also, while one application might appear similar to another, there could be a range of differing constraints and physical factors that are not immediately obvious but which could influence the decision. Where the circumstances of other applications are the same, there is some onus on councils and inspectors to reach the same decision. Councils often use the threat of setting an undesirable precedent to boost their reasons for refusing an application. At appeal, inspectors are often reluctant to pay much attention to precedent.

▶ Permitted development

The availability of permitted development rights to alter, enlarge or change the use of a building, without having to apply to the council for permission, should be taken into consideration. This is known as a 'fall-back' option. However, weight is not likely to be attached to it, unless there are reasonable prospects that the permitted development scheme might actually be built as an alternative to the scheme applied for.

▶ Benefits of a development

Some developments offer particular benefits for the community that can overcome policy objections. For example, a proposed housing scheme might offer much needed recreation space or an improvement to a dangerous road junction. Development might be proposed specifically to provide funding for the maintenance of a rundown listed building.

▶ Level of support or opposition

The level of support or opposition to a proposal is not in itself a material consideration, although a large body of supporters or objectors might have considerable political influence. Public opinion, though, can be material where it lends weight to a subjective judgment, for example on the merits of a particular design.

FACTORS NOT TAKEN INTO ACCOUNT

Factors that are not material considerations and, therefore, should not influence planning decisions include:

- loss of a private view;
- private legal matters, such as rights of way, covenants, and boundary disputes;
- effect on property values;
- possible future development;
- motives of applicants, including profit;
- applicant's conduct, personal affairs or how a business is run;
- disruption during building work;
- competition between businesses;
- morality and religious beliefs;
- aspects covered by other legislation, such as environmental health, party walls or building regulations.

The planning system is meant to operate in the public interest, and in an objective way, so these private matters are not supposed to be taken into account. That said, serious impacts of a private or personal nature might attract the sympathies of a planning officer or, more likely, a councillor, as could a history of antagonism with the council. These factors would be unlikely to be explicit yet could help tip a finely balanced decision so should not always be ignored entirely.

Focus points

✻ Decisions are based on development plan policies and material considerations.

✻ The principal policy sources are neighbourhood plans and local plans, each of which should be in line with national policy guidance.

✻ There is scope for public involvement in neighbourhood plans and local plans.

✻ Material considerations include a wide range of factors relevant to the development of land.

✻ Private matters are not material considerations.

Next step

With various policy and other considerations which go into planning decisions in mind, the next chapter looks at the decision process that planning applications go through.

The planning application process

In this chapter you will learn:

- ▶ *About the process for assessing planning applications*
- ▶ *About the process for making planning decisions*
- ▶ *What conditions may be imposed when planning permission is granted*
- ▶ *How the appeal process works*

The application process

The process for the assessment of planning applications is quite straightforward and involves a number of distinct steps. This chapter looks at that process; how to prepare an application and navigate through the system to best advantage is detailed in Part 2 and how to oppose an application is described in Part 3. A chart of the application process is set out in Figure 4.1.

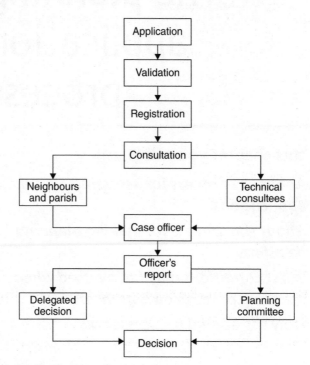

Figure 4.1 The planning application process

CHECKING AND VALIDATING

Once a planning application is received by the council it is checked to make sure it is complete. This involves ensuring the forms are correctly filled in, the necessary plans are provided, any required supporting documents are present and the correct fee has been paid. Councils publish validation checklists, which set out the information required for different types of application, and should only seek information that is absolutely necessary to decide an application. Some basic requirements are set nationally and others are left to the council to define locally. Examples of documents included in local validation checklists are:

- Additional plans and drawings
- Affordable housing statement
- Air quality assessment
- Biodiversity/ecological survey and report
- Environmental statement
- Flood risk assessment (FRA)
- Foul sewage and surface water assessment
- Heritage statement
- Highway statement
- Land contamination assessment
- Lighting assessment
- Noise impact assessment
- Open space assessment
- Planning obligations (legal undertaking) draft heads of terms
- Planning statement
- Statement of community involvement
- Structural survey
- Transport assessment
- Travel plan
- Tree and landscaping assessment
- Sustainability statement

Once it has been checked, the application is pronounced valid or, if it is considered incomplete, additional information is requested from the applicant. When an application is submitted in valid form, the date of registration should be the day or day after it is received, even if the validation process actually takes a week or more, as is sometimes the case. If additional information is sought, validation is usually delayed until the day, or day after, the additional information is received by the council.

Disputes over validation can result in an application not being registered. In England, applicants can serve a notice on the council, saying why they think the requested information is unnecessary. If the council agrees with the applicant, the application is validated; if it disagrees, the applicant has the right to appeal.

On validation, a letter is sent or emailed to the applicant (or the applicant's agent), giving the application reference, the date by which it should be determined and, usually, the name of the planning officer (known as the 'case officer') dealing with it. Basic details such as the site address and description of the proposal are included and should be checked to ensure they are correct. Most applications are supposed to be decided within eight weeks. Larger-scale applications, known as 'major' applications, should be dealt with within 13 weeks. Major applications include proposals for 10 or more houses, housing sites of 0.5 hectares or more, where the number of houses is not known, new floor space of 1,000 square metres or more, and sites of 1 hectare or more. All waste and minerals-related development is also classed as major.

The letter acknowledging the application does not guarantee the application is correct, as omissions or errors can emerge during the course of an application which could affect its validity.

Key idea

An application must be validated before it is considered by the council.

PUBLIC ACCESS TO APPLICATIONS

After a planning application is validated, it is placed on the planning register and enters the public realm. Councils make applications available to view via the planning application search facility on the planning pages of their websites and copies are available for inspection at their offices. All the forms, plans and supporting information can be seen by the public, including potential objectors, and also contractors and building materials suppliers who monitor applications then target applicants with their advertisements.

CONSULTATION

Following validation, the council starts a consultation exercise during which it notifies various parties that the application has been made and seeks their feedback on it. Consultees include the parish, town or community council, and advisors from both within and outside the council. In-house consultees might be the council's design or conservation officer, the tree or landscape officer and the environmental health department on matters of drainage and possible contamination. External consultation could involve the highway authority for comment on highway safety and parking, English Heritage if listed buildings are involved, and English Nature if protected species are potentially affected (or their equivalent bodies in other UK countries). The Environment Agency is consulted on flood risk and surface water drainage issues. Local interest groups such as historical or ecological societies could be consulted as well. Precisely who is consulted varies depending on the proposal. All consultees are given three weeks to respond to the council.

Parish councils, a term used here to cover parish, community and town councils, are consultees on applications. Some, though, have a planning committee, at which applications are considered, and this gives rise to confusion about their role. Parish councils cannot refuse or grant planning permission, they can only give their thoughts and a recommendation to the district council. Parish support or opposition can, though, influence district councillors and the planning committee, so should not be disregarded. Many parish councils allow members of the public to speak at their meetings when applications are considered. This can be a valuable opportunity for applicants to clarify the purpose and details of an application and to promote its merits (see Chapter 7). Similarly, objectors can attend such meetings and make known their concerns (see Chapter 11).

Key idea

A wide range of consultees is invited to comment on applications.

PUBLICITY

In addition to notifying the specific consultees, the council publicizes applications for public comment. Letters are sent to near neighbours setting out the application description, where and how details can be viewed and the timescale for responses. Although responses are sought within 21 days of notification, technically the council should take account of all responses received up to the date of the decision. Applications are published in a weekly list which is made available on the council's website and sometimes published in a local newspaper.

In addition, most councils post, or ask the applicant to post, a notice on the application site, saying what is proposed and giving a date by which comments can be sent to the council. It is not mandatory for applicants to display application notices, although councils are inclined to imply that it is. They sometimes come in eye-catching colours and so alert people to applications who might not otherwise be aware. Any member of the public can comment on an application, not just neighbours and those specifically notified by the council.

CASE OFFICER'S ASSESSMENT

At some stage during the course of the application, the case officer makes a site visit. This is frequently done unannounced. On occasion, objectors to a proposal ask the officer to come and look at the site from their properties to assess the impact and the officer might oblige. The case officer then considers responses from consultees, relevant development plan polices and any material considerations pertinent to the particular proposal, including the planning history. Although most applications run for eight weeks, it is not unusual for a case officer not to make an assessment of all the relevant factors until around six weeks or later into the process. Case officers do not have to follow the advice given to them by consultees but must have good reason to disregard technical expertise. If a decision goes against the advice of the Environment Agency on flood risk matters, the council must notify the Secretary of State for Communities and Local Government before the permission is issued.

CASE OFFICER'S REPORT AND RECOMMENDATION

The case officer's assessment is written up in a report which concludes with a recommendation for approval or refusal. The report details the proposal, planning history, relevant polices and responses from consultees. It then sets out the officer's assessment and recommendation. Reports can be short – no more than a side or two of A4 for straightforward or small-scale proposals – or lengthy, if the issues are more complex. If the recommendation is for approval, then suggested conditions are included in the report. If it is for refusal, draft reasons will be given. Some councils refer to 'balanced' recommendations where, essentially the planning officer is leaving the matter open to the planning committee to make a decision. Examples of typical headings in an officer's report are set out below:

► Introduction

► Consultation responses

► Site location and description

► The proposal

► Planning history

► Planning policy

► Evaluation

► Recommended decision and conditions/reasons

Key idea

The case officer's report summarizes his or her thinking on the application.

The decision process

DELEGATED DECISIONS

The majority of planning applications are decided by a delegated decision, where authority to take the decision is delegated from the councillors to a senior planning officer – usually a team leader or head of a planning department. The decision is taken following a review of the case officer's report by the senior officer. While decisions generally are made in line with the report, it is not unknown for applications to suffer a sudden reversal of fortunes at this late stage. There can be a very narrow time slot between an officer completing a report and the decision being issued, so there is scant opportunity for an applicant or objector to react to the recommendation if it is not to his or her liking.

PLANNING COMMITTEE DECISIONS

Different councils have different schemes of delegation for applications, that is, the rules governing which applications are decided by officers and which are put to committee. As a general rule, larger-scale developments are considered by committee, together with any that are particularly contentious. Where a district councillor asks for an application to go to committee, usually referred to as 'call in', this is generally allowed. Some councils have a timescale within which councillors' requests for a committee decision must be made. Others have a system where applications automatically go to committee when there are a certain number of objections, or where the officer's recommendation is contrary to the advice from the parish council.

Remember this

Find out if applicants or objectors can influence whether an application goes to planning committee.

When an application is to be decided by committee, the case officer's report is put on an agenda that becomes public at least five working days (in England) before the committee meeting, which usually means one week beforehand. The report is the basis for the committee's understanding and discussion of the case. It is not unknown for updates and addenda to the officer's report to be produced just before, or even at, a planning committee meeting.

A planning committee is a group of district councillors who meet in a public forum to discuss and decide planning applications. Most councils give applicants and objectors the opportunity to speak, although addresses to committee are usually limited to two or three minutes only. The general procedure for each application is a summary of the case from the planning officer, speeches (if any) by members of the public in support of or against the application, discussion among committee members and then a vote, where a simple majority decides the case. Some councils also allow councillors to ask those addressing the committee questions. Apart from that, applicants and interested parties generally have to sit and listen to the discussion without opportunity to intervene or contribute further. Suggestions on how to address a planning committee are given in Chapters 7 and 11.

In addition to refusing or approving planning applications, the committee can decide to defer a decision until a later date, pending the receipt of further information or, possibly, to allow a committee site visit to take place. The committee can pass a resolution to grant permission, subject to additional information being provided or a legal agreement being completed. In this latter scenario, the committee takes the decision, but the planning officer actually releases the planning permission at a later date when the outstanding matter has been dealt with. Where permission is to be granted, the committee might amend, remove or add to the conditions suggested in the officer's report. Similarly, the committee can add, alter or substitute reasons for refusal where an application is turned down.

DECISION NOTICE

Once the decision is made, either by the planning officer or committee, a decision notice is issued to the applicant and posted on the council's website. If permission is granted, the date of the decision is important, as the work or use must begin within a period of years (normally three), specified in the decision notice, from that date. The decision notice also sets out any conditions attached to the permission and usually lists the reference numbers of the approved drawings. Sometimes one or more 'informatives' are attached to the decision, clarifying some aspect of the permission or alerting the applicant to the need to obtain building regulations approval or other consents for the works.

Where the decision is refusal, again, the date on the notice is important as any appeal must be lodged within a certain time period from that date. The notice also sets out the reasons for refusal and should include information about how and when an appeal can be lodged. Example decision notices, for approval and refusal, are shown in Figures 4.2 and 4.3.

'CALLED IN' APPLICATIONS

Exceptionally, planning applications are taken out of the hands of the council before a decision is reached and the matter referred to what is essentially an appeal determined by public inquiry. This procedure is known as 'call-in'. Applications may be called in where:

▶ There is conflict with national policies on important matters.

▶ The proposal could have significant effects on meeting economic growth or housing needs beyond its immediate locality.

▶ There could be substantial national or regional controversy.

▶ There are significant architectural or urban design issues.

▶ Interests of national security or foreign governments are involved.

Even though called in applications go through a public inquiry procedure, the Secretary of State makes the decision and has to take the inquiry inspector's findings into consideration.

Town and Country Planning Act 1990

Notice of Decision
Application No. **BD/2013/1292/F**

**Binfield District
Council**

DESCRIPTION AND LOCATION OF DEVELOPMENT
**DEMOLITION OF EXISTING DWELLING AND ERECTION OF REPLACEMENT
BROOK END, MOODLEY LANE, EXTED PN21 6PU**

Binfield District Council, in pursuance of powers under the Town and Country
Planning Act 1990 (as amended), hereby **GRANTS PLANNING PERMISSION**
for the said proposals, subject to the conditions stated below imposed for the
reasons stated thereunder:-

1. The development to which this permission relates shall be begun not later
   than the expiration of three years beginning with the date on which this permission
   is granted.

   REASON: To meet the requirements of Section 51 of the Planning and
   Compulsory Purchase Act 2004.

2. Before any groundworks take place for the development hereby approved, details
   of the form and position of fencing, which shall comply in full with BS5837:2012
   'Trees in relation to design, demolition & construction – Recommendations', for
   the protection of those trees, shrubs and natural features not scheduled for removal
   shall be submitted to and be to the written approval of the Local Planning Authority,
   and such fencing shall be erected in the positions approved before the development
   is commenced and thereafter retained until such completion of the development, to
   the approval of the Local Planning Authority. Hereafter, the fencing shall be referred
   to as the 'approved protection zone'.

   REASON: To preserve trees and hedges on the site in the interests of visual
   amenity and the character of the area, having regard to Policies EN8, EN12 and
   EN14 of the adopted Binfield Local Plan, coupled with paragraphs 109, 117 and
   118 of the National Planning Policy Framework 2012.

3. Before construction of the dwelling hereby approved, samples of materials
   and finishes to be used on the external surfaces of the development, including
   window, balustrade and hard surface treatment, shall be made available for
   inspection on site and adequate notice given to the Local Planning Authority who
   will arrange inspection and thereafter confirm in writing. The approved materials
   shall be used in the implementation of the development.

   REASON: To safeguard the appearance of the premises and the character of the
   area generally and to enable the Local Planning Authority to properly consider
   and control the development, having regard to Saved Policies EN8 and EN27 of
   the adopted Binfield Local Plan, coupled with the requirements of paragraph
   56, 57, 59, 60, 64 and 109 of the National Planning Policy Framework 2012.

Figure 4.2 Example of decision notice granting permission

4. Before the first occupation of the building hereby permitted the en suite window at first floor on the north east elevation shall be fitted with obscure-glazing and shall be permanently retained in that condition thereafter.

REASON: To safeguard the privacy of the occupiers of the adjoining property having regard to Saved Policy EN27 of the adopted Binfield Local Plan, coupled with the requirements of paragraph 17 of the National Planning Policy Framework 2012.

5. Notwithstanding the provisions of The Town and Country Planning (General Permitted Development) (Amendment) (No. 2) (England) Order 2008 (or any Order revoking and re-enacting that Order with or without modification), no buildings, structures or works as defined within Part 1 of Schedule 2, classes A–D inclusive of that Order, shall be erected or undertaken on the site otherwise than in accordance with a planning permission granted by the Local Planning Authority.

REASON: To enable the Local Planning Authority to regulate and control the development of land having regard to Policies GD2, EN8, EN27 and DC18 of the adopted Wealden Local Plan, coupled with the requirements of paragraphs 17, 56 and 109 of the National Planning Policy Framework 2012.

10. This planning decision relates solely to the following plan(s):

Ref. Date Stamped. STN4

PE1 16 July 2013
PE2 16 July 2013
X01 A 16 July 2013
X02 A 16 July 2013

REASON: For the avoidance of doubt.

DATE OF ISSUE: 10 May 2014

A Cadaver
Head of Planning & Environmental Services

Figure 4.2 (*Continued*)

Town and Country Planning Act, 1990

REFUSAL

Winshire District Council

REFERENCE: 13/03684/FUL

DESCRIPTION: **Construction of detached dwelling with associated landscaping works, to the side of 'Woodfields' with new driveway access and parking areas to serve the new dwelling.**

LOCATION: Woodfields, Furfilled Road, East Grinmore, Winshire

DECISION DATE: 7 Jun 2014

The Council hereby notify you that they **REFUSE** to permit the above development as shown in the submitted application and plans.

The reasons for the Council's decision are:

1. The proposed development by virtue of its design, layout and loss of vegetation, would detract from the character of the area and would be prejudicial to the character of the Furfilled Road Area of Townscape Character. The application therefore conflicts with Policies B1, B16 and H3 of the Mid Winshire Local Plan and the policies of the National Planning Policy Framework 2012.

2. The proposed development would give rise to an unacceptable loss of privacy to the adjoining property Hill Crest, due to overlooking of principal room windows. The application conflicts with Policy H4 of the Mid Winshire Local Plan.

INFORMATIVES

1. You are advised that the District Council determined this application on the basis of the following drawings:

   1.01/A
   051.01/A
   2.01/A
   2.02/A

Figure 4.3 Example of decision notice refusing planning permission

Conditions

Planning permission is generally granted subject to conditions. These are limitations which can be put on when and how the development is carried out, how it is used, future changes to buildings and requirements for further information to be submitted. Government guidance sets out six tests which conditions should pass. These are that conditions should be:

▶ necessary

▶ relevant to planning

▶ relevant to the development to be permitted

▶ enforceable

▶ precise

▶ reasonable in all other respects.

How many conditions and what topics are covered depends on the nature of the development and the amount of detail included with the application. For something simple, like a house extension, you might only find the standard time-limiting condition, which is three years (five years in Wales and Northern Ireland). For a new house, typically, conditions require samples of materials to be submitted, a landscaping scheme, drainage details and parking and access arrangements to be put in place in advance of building the house. Common planning conditions imposed by councils are set out below:

▶ standard time limit

▶ samples or details of materials to be submitted and approved

▶ landscaping scheme to be submitted and approved

▶ drainage information to be submitted and approved

▶ parking and access arrangements to be submitted and approved

▶ construction to achieve specified code level under code for sustainable homes

▶ specified windows to be obscure-glazed

- hours of construction
- removal or restriction of permitted development rights
- development to be carried out in accordance with approved plans

Some conditions require further information to be submitted and approved by the council. This involves a simple application where a short form has to be completed and a fee paid, before the information is considered by the council. Conditions might entail such additional information being approved before the building works start or before the building is occupied. Where details required are not agreed by the council, there is scope to appeal.

Planning agreements and the Community Infrastructure Levy

In addition to conditions, planning permission can be granted subject to the applicant first signing a legally binding undertaking, often referred to as a 'planning agreement' or 'Section 106 Agreement' (Section 75 in Scotland and Article 40 in Northern Ireland) with the council. Agreements can cover financial contributions required by the council or the provision of affordable housing in residential developments. Councils also use agreements to control a wide range of other factors, such as restricting the occupancy of a building, preventing a building being sold off from adjoining land or buildings (known as a 'non-severance' agreement) or as a way of ensuring some benefit arising from a development, like a new road or community facility, is delivered.

Planning agreements are legal documents that become local land charges when completed. This means they attach to the land ownership and not to the parties who signed them. Consequently, it is important that agreements are correctly drawn up and, although councils often produce templates for them, it is nonetheless advisable to use a solicitor to make sure an agreement is satisfactory. This adds cost and councils also usually charge applicants their own legal costs. Agreements can also add to the time pressure in making a planning application as councils generally expect the document to be signed within the 8- or 13-week target time period for making a decision. For larger developments, agreements are sometimes finalized after the council has passed a resolution to grant permission when the details are settled through the two sides' lawyers.

To bring about greater consistency in the payment of financial contributions, the government in England and Wales introduced the Community Infrastructure Levy, or CIL. While adoption of CIL is not compulsory, most councils are, at the time of writing, putting it in place.

CIL provisions are complex, with reliefs and exceptions, including one which takes conversions out of the scope of the levy if they do not create new floor space. CIL is levied in pounds per square metre of floor space and applies to all new dwellings and to extensions over 100 square metres, including any of that size which are built as permitted development, without the need to apply for planning permission. A replacement dwelling should be charged on the additional space created. Payment is triggered by the commencement of the development. Rates are set locally and vary considerably among those councils that charge the CIL. (At the time of writing, there is an intention to remove single, self-built houses and residential extensions or annexes from CIL liability.) Unlike planning agreements, there are no legal fees or delays to the granting of planning permission.

Key idea

The grant of planning permission can trigger a requirement to pay the Community Infrastructure Levy or make a financial contribution to the council.

Reasons for refusal

When planning permission is refused, the council must give reasons and those reasons must be related to relevant planning policies. Reasons for refusal vary in style from one long rambling paragraph to short numbered sentences covering different topics. Reasons for refusal might concern the very principle of the proposal or detailed aspects of it. This distinction is important, as objections to points of detail could be the subject of follow-up negotiations and amendments to the proposal, to render it acceptable. A resubmission of an application can be done without paying a second application fee, subject to criteria including that the proposed scheme is of a similar nature and on the same site as the original. This 'free go' provision applies for 12 months from the decision date.

> **Remember this**
>
> When an application is refused, it might be possible to get a 'free go' to reapply within 12 months of the decision.

Right of appeal

After a planning application, and most other types of application, has been made, an appeal can be lodged against the refusal of the application, against particular conditions attached to a planning permission or against the council's failure to validate a planning application or to make a decision within the statutory target time period. The latter two situations are known as 'non-determination' appeals. Only the person who made the application can make an appeal.

Appeals have to be made within six months of the date of the decision notice or, in non-determination cases, within six months of the target date for the council to make a decision (three months in either case in Scotland). For appeals against householder planning application refusals in England and Wales, the time limit is within 12 weeks of a decision. Time periods differ where an enforcement notice has been served.

Appeals are administered by the Planning Inspectorate in England and Wales, the Directorate of Planning and Environmental Appeals in Scotland, and the Planning Appeals Commission in Northern Ireland. These are central government agencies, independent of district councils. Decisions, in nearly all cases, are taken by an inspector in England and Wales, a reporter in Scotland or a commissioner in Northern Ireland. Scotland has a slightly different system in which decisions on small-scale proposals are subject to review rather than appeal (see below).

Key idea

There are strict time limits within which to lodge a planning appeal.

The appeal methods and processes

Appeals can be decided by three different methods, known as written representations, hearings and public inquiries. In England and Wales, the Planning Inspectorate decides which method should be adopted, although the person making the appeal can express a preference. All appeals start with the completion of a form (notice of appeal) which establishes who is appealing and the site address and application details. The person appealing, called the 'appellant', has to attach copies of all the planning application documents, including the council's decision notice, and a statement of the grounds, or basis, for making the appeal. A copy of the appeal form and grounds of appeal must also be sent to the council. At the time of writing there are no statutory fees for appeals.

On receipt, appeals are checked for completeness and then a start letter is sent to the appellant and council. This sets out the timetable for the appeal, the appeal reference and the name of the case officer who will administer the appeal. The appeal inspector, who makes the decision, is not appointed at this stage. Neither the appellant nor the council can liaise directly with the inspector in any case.

Councils publicize appeals by notifying all those who commented on the original planning application. Those original representations are sent to the appeal inspector by the council, but additional comments can be submitted as well.

Anybody can comment on an appeal, regardless of whether they commented on the original application.

WRITTEN REPRESENTATIONS

The majority of appeals are determined by this method. It involves the appellant submitting grounds of appeal, which is a statement setting out the reasons why permission should be granted. The council then has the opportunity to present its case, within a specified number of weeks of the start of the appeal. In addition to its arguments, the council must set out any conditions it would like to see imposed by the inspector, should the appeal be allowed. These conditions are given without prejudice to the council's position that the appeal should be dismissed. Each side can then comment on the other's case, on the suggested conditions and on any representations from third parties (members of the public). A site visit is then arranged, when the inspector looks at the site and its surroundings. Where a site cannot be clearly seen from adjoining roads, the inspection is attended by the appellant and/or his or her agent, if one is appointed, and a planning officer from the council. The parties cannot discuss the appeal with the inspector. Objectors can attend but, again, cannot make any representations. If a site can be clearly seen from public places, the inspector makes the visit unaccompanied. The appeal decision letter is sent out anything between a few days and a month following the site visit.

HEARING

The procedure for a hearing is similar to written representations, except at the end of the process, usually on the same day as the site visit, the inspector sits down with the appellant and planning officer to discuss the case. Members of the public can attend as well to have their say. The procedure is relatively informal, with the inspector raising discussion points and seeking the views of the parties. During the site visit the discussion is usually able to continue, unlike the procedure for written representations.

PUBLIC INQUIRY

A public inquiry is a more formal procedure, where each side formally presents its case and can be cross-examined by the other party. Members of the public can speak and can be cross-examined by the main parties. Most appellants have professional representation and it is common for barristers to be involved, acting as advocates for each side. There is a site visit, either after or during the inquiry, and the inquiry may remain open during the visit, so that pertinent issues can be addressed by the parties and the inspector can ask questions.

HOUSEHOLDER APPEALS (ENGLAND AND WALES)

Householder appeals have an abbreviated procedure and are supposed to be dealt with much more quickly than standard written appeals, within eight weeks from lodging the appeal to the decision. Only the application form and application decision has to be submitted at the outset, together with brief grounds of appeal. There is no scope for the council or members of the public to make representations or to respond to the grounds of appeal.

LOCAL REVIEW (SCOTLAND)

Where a decision in Scotland is a delegated one, made by planning officers, in respect of a development classified by the council concerned as 'local', there is no right of appeal to Scottish ministers. Instead, the applicant can request a review by submitting a form within three months of the decision. The proposed development is considered by a local review board, which is a committee of at least three councillors. The review board can decide the case on the notice of review form and application documents, require written submissions, hold a hearing session, carry out a site inspection or a combination of these. The review board's decision is final.

APPEAL DECISIONS

In all cases, appeal decisions are in the form of a letter explaining what the inspector considers to be the key issues and his or her findings on those issues. If the appeal is allowed (succeeds), the decision letter is the planning permission and will include any conditions the inspector deems necessary. If an appeal is dismissed (unsuccessful), it is important to look carefully at the inspector's findings to determine the precise reasons. It is possible that the inspector disagreed with some of the reasons for refusal or only dismissed the appeal on one point of detail. In these circumstances, if a revised application is made to the council which overcomes the inspector's concerns, the council is expected to take notice of the inspector's reasoning in reaching a new decision.

COSTS

The general rule with planning appeals is that each side bears its own costs. There is, however, provision for an award of costs to be made in the exceptional circumstances where one side has acted unreasonably. What represents unreasonable behaviour is set out in some detail in government guidance. Situations that commonly give rise to successful costs claims by both appellants and councils are shown in Table 4.1.

Table 4.1 Typical situations where costs are awarded at appeal

Against the appellant	Against the council
Appeal proposal clearly contrary to policy	Ignoring consultees' advice without good reason
Recent dismissed appeal for something similar	Refusing something clearly supported by policy
Introducing new material that should have been in the planning application	Failing to provide adequate evidence to support reasons for refusal
Failing to attend appeal site visit	Withdrawing a reason for refusal
Not providing a legal agreement where one is clearly needed	Ignoring a recent allowed appeal for something similar
Withdrawing the appeal without good reason	Failing to attend appeal site visit

Key idea

Costs are rarely awarded in planning appeals and only where there is 'unreasonable behaviour'.

Focus points

* Once validated and registered, planning applications are in the public realm.
* Consultees and the public feed back technical advice and local opinion to application case officers.
* Applications are decided by planning officers under delegated powers or by a planning committee.
* Permission is granted subject to conditions.
* Refusal, non-determination and onerous conditions can all be the subject of an appeal.

Next step

Part 1 has explained what the planning system is, the situations where permission is required and the basis and mechanism for making application and appeal decisions. The question for applicants is, then, how best to use that system to obtain planning permission. Part 2 sets out the practical steps to take before, during and after a planning application to ensure an optimum outcome for a project.

PART 2

MAKING PLANNING
APPLICATIONS

Before making your application

In this chapter you will learn:

▶ *How to check whether you need to submit an application*

▶ *About pre-application consultations*

▶ *How talking to neighbours, and parish and district councillors can improve your chances of getting planning permission*

▶ *How to find relevant information and guidance*

▶ *When to seek professional advice*

▶ *How to prepare your property*

Checking what applications are needed

For the reasons explained in Chapter 2, not all work and changes of use require a planning application to be submitted. Consider whether your scheme is:

▶ sufficiently minor that it would not be deemed to be 'development' at all;

▶ within the scope of permitted development rights;

▶ allowed by a neighbourhood development order;

▶ permitted by a local development order;

▶ covered by a previous planning permission which has not lapsed or has been implemented.

If you think an application is not necessary, assuming the project you propose will involve some effort and cost, it is worth getting confirmation that a planning application (or other type of application, such as for listed building consent) is not required. There are several ways to do this.

First, you can ask an officer at the council. Just phoning up a receptionist or a planning officer on phone duty and getting an off-the-cuff verbal view is unreliable. As you might have surmised, planning law and regulations are complicated with many ifs, buts and maybes. It would be easy for an officer not to appreciate some vital factor which could make a difference. Councils are not bound by what officers say and, of course, there would not even be a record of what was said over the phone. At least go in to the council's offices, taking drawings or photos, to discuss the proposal. You can make use of the council's pre-application consultation regime (see below). If you are told no applications are needed, ask for written confirmation. Having a letter or email does not prevent the council changing its mind but it is less likely to happen.

Second, you can make an application for a lawful development certificate (see Chapter 2). The process is similar to a planning application in that there are forms to complete, drawings to get prepared and a fee to pay the council. If a lawful development certificate is issued, providing you stick to the proposal presented to the council, you will have the comfort of a formal confirmation that the project can go ahead. Bear in mind that a lawful development certificate establishes only that a planning application is not necessary at the time it is issued. Changes in law, regulations or other circumstances can affect the need for permission. An advantage of lawful development certificates is that the council should not refuse to issue one if it or the neighbours do not like what is proposed. The decision is meant to be based purely on whether it comes within the relevant law and rules. Remember that a few permitted development rights involve the prior notification of the council (see Chapter 2) and there are separate, relatively simple application processes for this.

Third, you can get a professional opinion. It is important to stress 'professional' as builders and contractors are sometimes quite free with their opinions on whether consents are needed but the rules are many and complicated and you might have little recourse should their advice prove wrong. Professionals, such as planning consultants and lawyers, have indemnity insurance. No matter who you consult, it is only the council (or a planning inspector at appeal) which has the power to say definitively whether permission is required.

Remember this

Check whether and what applications are needed.

If you believe or find out that an application is necessary, check with the council precisely what type of application is appropriate in the circumstances. It could, for example, be a full planning application, an outline application, a householder application, an application to remove or vary a condition, a minor amendment application or a listed building or Conservation Area consent application. Outline applications are generally made when you wish to test the principle of development, for example, whether a site is suitable to accommodate a new house or where you intend getting permission and selling the site. This avoids the need to have detailed drawings prepared before you know whether a building will be allowed at all or what prospective purchasers might want to build.

Pre-application consultations

Most councils have a pre-application consultation regime in place whereby prospective applicants can get an initial view from planning officers on their proposals, prior to submitting a planning application. In Scotland, the term 'pre-application consultation' refers to consultation with the local community and enquiries to officers are referred to as 'pre-application advice'. The latter expression is also often used in other UK countries but the term 'consultation' is used in this book so as not to confuse it with independent professional advice.

Pre-application consultations can be of the old fashioned variety, where you can ring up the planning department, arrange a meeting on site or at the council's offices or call in to the councils' offices and see a duty planning officer or, maybe, any officer who happens to be available. That is rare now and most councils have some kind of formal system in place. This might involve making an appointment for a brief meeting with a duty planning officer, completing a form and providing specified information such as draft drawings and outline statements, or arranging a meeting with an officer and, sometimes, councillors as well. Some regimes are sufficiently onerous that it is actually easier to make a planning application than it is to use the consultation process. Most councils have a section on their website which sets out how the pre-application consultation system works. Alternatively, a phone call to the planning department should elicit how your council handles such consultations. Various scales of development are often dealt with differently.

Councils usually make a charge for pre-application consultations; each council sets its own level. The charge can vary depending on the type of project, the chosen method of response (e.g. a letter or a meeting), and which officers need to attend or contribute. Some charges are so exorbitant that it is cheaper to make a speculative planning application.

Remember this

You can get a good idea about the likely success of your project by carrying out pre-application consultation.

There are several advantages to carrying out a pre-application consultation. If, in principle, your proposal stands almost no chance of success, finding out early can save you wasting time and money on it. Taking account of the planning officer's views should enhance the prospects of your application being approved. The officer should draw your attention to the relevant policies and standards to help you design or refine your project. The officer can tell you which type of application(s) is appropriate, and what documents and information would be necessary in the application.

On the other hand, pre-application consultations have their limits. Council officers do not give independent professional advice. Depending on the integrity of the officer, you might be given the council's party line rather than an objective assessment. There is very little redress if you are given incorrect information or the response is vague and/or non-committal. The views of the officer are not binding on the council so there is no guarantee that what you are told, even when it is in writing, will carry through to the decision on your application. The pre-application consultation might be carried out by a junior officer, who is susceptible to being overruled by a senior officer. Some officers seem to make a habit of rowing back when a planning application is made after a positive pre-application response. Unlike planning applications, pre-application consultations are not subject to statutory timescales against which the performance of councils is measured. Consequently, planning officers have an incentive to prioritize dealing with applications ahead of consultations.

If your project warrants a pre-application consultation, ascertain your council's regime from its website or planning department.

Ask how long responses are actually taking, as opposed to the quoted target timescale. Decide whether you feel a meeting could be more productive than a letter, perhaps because you want to discuss various options. Send the specified information to the council, following its procedures. Where a meeting is to be held, do not wait for the officer to contact you, try phoning them to make an appointment. In any event, contact the officer early on to check that they have all the necessary information and the project is clear. Ask the officer when the response is likely to be forthcoming and always request the response to be confirmed in writing. Follow this up with an email or phone call if you do not hear within the stated period.

Remember this

Use what the planning officer says in your supporting application statement.

Neighbours

The most likely source of objection to a planning application is the people living closest to the property. While the existence of one or more objections does not mean an application will be refused, it is better not to have any. Also, consulting the people potentially affected by development is a neighbourly thing to do. On some occasions, neighbours object because they do not understand what is being proposed. There is a tendency for people to be, at best, suspicious, not to say fearful, of change in their environment. Potentially, a good deal of this can be avoided by speaking to neighbours before making your application and, ideally, before finalizing the proposal.

Remember this

Talking to neighbours increases the chances of getting planning permission.

Consulting nearby residents is a matter to be judged in each case and depends on the nature of your relationship with them. If you are on good terms, you could raise the matter when it is just an idea to test the water. When you start to get draft drawings prepared, you could pop around and discuss the proposal over a cup of tea. On the other hand, if you suspect a neighbour will object regardless of what is proposed, or you do not have a harmonious relationship with a neighbour, it might be best not to risk making matters worse. An early warning of an application gives a neighbour the opportunity to organize his or her opposition and lobby other neighbours in advance.

How far afield to consult will be dependent on the scale and potential impact of the project. In the case of a rear extension, speaking to the neighbours on each side is probably all that is necessary. If you are proposing to build a new house, maybe a few households in either direction on each side of the road and a few properties at the rear would be appropriate. If you do not know the neighbours, or would not be comfortable with knocking on doors, you could prepare a short note introducing the idea – with or without a copy of a drawing – and post it through the letter boxes.

In a meeting with neighbours, explain what is proposed and point out how you have taken their interests into account, such as preserving their outlook or avoiding windows looking into their gardens. Many people are unused to reading drawings so ensure they understand what you are proposing, perhaps taking them outside to show them where walls, windows and so on will be located. Ask whether they have any concerns, bearing in mind people's tendency not to wish to appear impolite. If a neighbour does raise something, consider whether there could be an amendment which would overcome the perceived problem, for example setting a wall further from a boundary, re-positioning a window or relocating an access point. Obviously, you will have to weigh up whether or not you would be prepared to change your design to accommodate a neighbour's concern. You could follow up any revisions with a second meeting to ensure the neighbour is content.

When neighbours say they are perfectly happy with the scheme, you can take things a step further and find out whether they would be prepared to actively support your proposal, when submitted. This would involve them writing a letter expressing their approval of what you are planning to do, ready for submission with the application or, alternatively, sent on to the council after submission (see Chapter 7). Despite their best intentions, people can be slow to put pen to paper so think about offering to draft a letter for the neighbour to sign. If you are doing this for several neighbours, as far as possible, put the letter in the individual neighbour's words rather than producing a standard text and asking several households to sign it. Support which looks too manufactured might carry less weight.

Make a note of any contact you have with neighbours. This can be usefully added to your planning application supporting letter or statement (see Chapter 6).

Policy documents and guidance

Where you have carried out a pre-application consultation, the planning officer should have pointed you towards any relevant planning policies and standards. Otherwise, the policies will be in documents available on the council's website or at its offices. However, the number and type of policy documents, and the planning jargon used to describe them, can make it fiendishly complicated to ascertain which policies are in force and which apply to any particular area or proposal. Since policies are the starting point for a decision, they are important. If you have not been told already, phone the planning department to ask which documents, policies and guidelines you need to know about. The council's defences might not allow you to speak to a development management officer (one who deals with planning applications) and it is often easier to get hold of a planning policy officer.

Finding your property on the proposals map should alert you to any special planning designations which apply to the area, such as a Conservation Area. You can look up the policies and guidance for your area and project type to see how your scheme measures up. If there is relevant guidance, for example, for house and extension design (see Chapter 3), it is likely to be more specific and tangible than planning policies. The latter can be very vague and rely on subjective judgements, such as requiring 'good design'. Policy and guidance can be referred to in a supporting letter or statement (see Chapter 6). If it appears your proposal would fall foul of a policy or guideline, go back to the planning officer to discuss it or take professional advice (see below).

In addition to guidance on development itself, councils publish guidance on making applications and on its application processes. It is a good idea to read this. While many of the regulations are set by national government, and so will be standard throughout the country, there is leeway in some areas and it can be useful to know your council's peculiarities. An example is which applications are decided by planning officers and which are decided by the planning committee.

One document to look out for in particular is the validation checklist. This list of information which might be required to accompany a planning application is partly prescribed nationally and partly set locally by each council. Councils publish their checklists on their websites and have copies at their offices. What kind of information has to be submitted varies according to the scale of the project, the nature of the area in which the property is located and the type of development proposed. A sample local list of information is given in Chapter 4. Generally speaking, it is only larger developments which necessitate significant additional reports to be prepared (see Chapter 6). A single new house or works to an existing residential property often will not need anything beyond the standard application requirements.

Remember this

Find out early what additional information might be required so you can get it organized to prevent delays.

If you carry out a pre-application consultation, ask the planning officer which, if any, items from the validation checklist the council would seek with your application. Otherwise, it is a good idea to phone the council and ask which documents it requires. Councils are supposed to be reasonable in their requests for information but that does not stop some exhibiting an over-zealous, tick-box mentality.

Contacting parish and district councillors

Where there is a parish, town or community council, they will be consulted about your planning application. While they do not have the power to dictate the decision, in some areas they do have influence. Sounding out parish councillors can, therefore, be helpful. Most proposals are uncontentious and raise little interest and it is unnecessary to approach the parish council about them. Where, though, you suspect your scheme might be controversial or the district council planning officers indicate they are likely to oppose it, it can be worth speaking to the parish council in advance of an application. Parish councils have clerks and, unless you know one of the councillors, they are usually the best first point of contact. Some parish councils are happy for you to contact councillors; others restrict contact with councillors to speaking at public parish council meetings. You might be asked to go along to a meeting to introduce your proposal and the councillors will discuss it and give their views. You might find that your only opportunity to explain your project is to address the parish council once your planning application has been submitted (see Chapter 7).

District councillors, ultimately, are the people with the power to decide planning applications. Seeking some early feedback could help shape your project or decide whether to pursue it at all. A large majority of applications are decided by planning officers and might well never come to the attention of the councillors. As with contacting parish councils, with most proposals it is inappropriate to contact district councillors. In fact, if your project is likely to sail through as a delegated decision, drawing a district councillor's attention to it could prove counter-productive. You do have the option to wait until after submission before deciding whether to contact councillors (see Chapter 7). District councils have varying rules about contact with councillors. Some are very worried about appearing not to be impartial and unbiased. In these areas, any pre-application contact can be discouraged. In other areas, councillors join planning officers in pre-application meetings.

Key idea

The support of councillors can overcome any planning officers' objections to your proposal.

Where you do contact parish or district councillors pre-application, note what they say and consider whether there is scope to revise your plans, should there be any concerns.

Professional help

Planning applications can be straightforward, especially relatively small-scale domestic ones. They can, though, be complex, with further complications added by some unhelpful or inefficient officers and/or councils. It is often unpredictable at the outset which your proposal will prove to be. There are various professionals to whom you can turn for help. Where you are going to use a professional, it is worthwhile having them involved at the beginning of the process. They can advise on what is practical, whether an application is required and if so what type, and the prospects for obtaining permission.

Planning applications involving new build work or new buildings will require drawings (see Chapter 6). Unless the work is simple and you have adequate drawing skills, you will need to get these prepared professionally. It is best to use someone who is familiar not only with building design and planning applications, but with building regulations and construction as well, in order to ensure that whatever is submitted can be built practically. There are various professionals who produce drawings, including architects, building surveyors and technicians. The term 'architect' is often used to describe anyone who designs or supervises building but, properly, describes officially registered architects. The main qualifications to look out for are ARIBA (architects), MRICS (chartered surveyors) and MCIAT (architectural technologists). You can elect to get drawings prepared and make the application yourself, if you wish, although designers generally complete and submit the application for you.

Remember this

Using a professional maximizes your chances of an application getting permission.

If early indications from the council or neighbours are that an application will be difficult, your designer advises you to do so or there is a great deal at stake, you can use a planning specialist to help you. Planning consultants deal with the technicalities of planning applications and policies, and the planning system generally. The main qualifications are MRICS (chartered planning and development surveyors) and MRTPI (chartered town planner). A planning consultant can advise on the chances of success and how to approach an application, recommend designers, manage the application or prepare a planning statement. You do not have to hand the whole application over to a planning consultant and can, if you choose, just commission a supporting letter or statement.

You are not obliged to use a professionally qualified designer or planning consultant. While professional qualifications do not guarantee a good job, they do indicate a level of competence and the possibility of redress should things go awry.

There are a range of other consultants you might need to bring on board depending on the circumstances. This is covered in Chapter 6.

Preparing the property

Having looked into your proposal, carried out pre-application consultation and/or taken professional advice, the matters which are likely to be or could potentially be issues in the assessment and decision of an application should become apparent. Where it is clear that a feature of the existing property, the nature of the proposal or aspects of adjoining properties could cause a problem, you might be able to take action in advance of submitting an application in order to maximize its chances of success.

Where there is potential for loss of privacy, a fence could be erected or trees planted to provide screening. Hedges or fences currently blocking visibility at an access point could be removed or reduced in height. This could include obstacles on adjoining land, providing you first secure the consent of the landowner. Trees in the way of new building can be felled. Shrubs, overgrowth or buildings can be cleared to open up a site so that the amount of space available is more apparent. If an application is to be made for a new house in a garden, the site could be fenced off to make the proposed division clear and the building plot more obvious. Where a new building or extension might be considered prominent or stark, you can get screen planting underway and allow it to establish. A secondary window could be blocked up to head off a reduction-in-outlook argument.

In most cases, pre-emptive preparation is not necessary. Should you feel it would or might be helpful, however, ensure that the work concerned does not itself need permission of any kind. In particular, check for tree preservation orders, Conservation Area designations or conditions on previous planning permission before felling or pruning trees. Remember demolition in Conservation Areas can require consent. Also bear in mind that the removal of existing buildings or other features on a site can be used as a bargaining point to justify a new building or greater extent of building than would otherwise be allowed. Once the building or feature has gone, the fact it was once there might well not carry any weight.

Focus points

* Check what applications are needed. Carry out pre-application consultations.
* Consider speaking to neighbours, and parish and district councillors.
* Look at planning policy documents.
* Decide what professional help to get, such as a planning consultant or designer.
* Prepare your property to increase the chances of success.

Next step

Following the steps in this chapter prepares the ground for your planning application so you are ready to move with confidence to preparing the application documentation for submission to the council.

Making your planning application

In this chapter you will learn:

▶ *How to complete and submit your application*
▶ *What drawings to include*
▶ *How to put forward your case in an accompanying letter or statement*
▶ *What additional information may be required*

Online and paper applications

Except in Northern Ireland, planning applications can be made over the internet and most are now made in this way. In England and Wales, online applications are made via the Planning Portal website, while in Scotland the ePlanning Scotland website provides the same service. These are run on behalf of the respective national governments and there are links to them from council websites. In addition to facilitating online applications, there is information about the process. In order to make applications via these websites, you have to first create an account with them and then enter your username and password to continue.

Online submission enables forms, certificates and notices to be completed, documents (in electronic form) to be attached and application fees to be paid. When making an application over the internet, you do not have to submit all documents by that means. The form and certificates can be completed online, while some or all documents and/or a cheque to cover the application fee can be posted. Guidance is available while you are completing the form, and the system flags up any parts of the form that have not been filled in. Applications can be begun and saved partially completed allowing you to go back and finish them later. The process is not particularly complicated but, like all computer-based systems, there are occasional peculiarities. Also, real life does not always fit conveniently into pre-determined categories. There is limited scope for deviating from the standard format if the answer to a question is not as straightforward as 'yes' or 'no'. An online application avoids the need to provide multiple paper copies of written documents and drawings, and having to post or take them to the council's offices. Applications made this way can be submitted on any day of the week and at any time of day and cannot be lost in the post.

If you are only ever likely to make one planning application in your life, or computers are not your strong suit and there is no one to help you, it might not be worth registering and working out how to use the online system.

The alternative is to make your application using paper forms. These can be downloaded from the council's website or via the Planning Portal or ePlanning Scotland. The forms can also be obtained from the council's planning department. If you are ordering forms by phone or visiting the council's officer to collect them, the staff should be able to help you to indentify which forms, certificates and notices are required for your project. Depending on who you speak to, you might also get some guidance on completing them. You will need to get the appropriate number of copies of the completed forms and drawings to submit. Large drawings can be relatively expensive to get copied. One advantage of applying on paper is the ability to write in more information than a question demands or to clarify an answer.

Completing application forms

The questions to be answered vary with the nature of the proposal, whether you apply for full or outline planning permission and whether listed building and/or Conservation Area consent is also being sought but much is common to all planning applications. There are guidance notes which accompany each form and it is a good idea to have these to hand when filling it in. Should you get stuck, refer to the online guidance or speak to a planning officer. Some questions are simple enough to answer and/or the standard guidance is clear. Following Figure 6.1 are questions, based on the standard forms for England (see Figure 6.1), where there can be further considerations.

Householder Application for Planning Permission for works or extension to a dwelling.
Town and Country Planning Act 1990

1. Applicant Name, Address and Contact Details

Title: Mr & Mrs   First name: F   Surname: Evans

Company name:

Street address: 17 Wentworth Drive

	Country Code	National Number	Extension Number
Telephone number:		01887674392	
Mobile number:			

Town/City: Highstock

County:

Country:

Postcode: GN6 &NH

Fax number:

Email address: evans@email.co.uk

Are you an agent acting on behalf of the applicant?   ○ Yes ● No

2. Agent Name, Address and Contact Details

No Agent details were submitted for this application

3. Description of Proposed Works

Please describe the proposed works:

Erection of a side and rear extension

Has the work already been started without planning permission?   ○ Yes ● No

4. Site Address Details

Full postal address of the site (including full postcode where available)   Description:

House: 17   Suffix:

House name:

Street address: Wentworth Drive

Town/City: Highstock

County:

Postcode: GN6 7NH

Description of location or a grid reference (must be completed if postcode is not known):

Easting: 530760

Northing: 115790

5. Pedestrian and Vehicle Access, Roads and Rights of Way

Is a new or altered vehicle access proposed to or from the public highway?   ○ Yes ● No

Is a new or altered pedestrian access proposed to or from the public highway?   ○ Yes ● No

Do the proposals require any diversions, extinguishment and/or creation of public rights of way?   ○ Yes ● No

6. Pre-application Advice

Has assistance or prior advice been sought from the local authority about this application?   ● Yes ○ No

If Yes, please complete the following information about the advice you were given (this will help the authority to deal with this application more efficiently):

Officer name:

Title: First name: Jeremy   Surname: Grunge

Reference: 2314/15

Date (DD/MM/YYYY): 10/05/2014   (Must be pre-application submission)

Details of the pre-application advice received:

Subject to setting back the front elevation, the proposal should be acceptable

Figure 6.1 A standard planning application form for England (Planning Portal © Crown copyright)

7. Trees and Hedges

Are there any trees or hedges on your own property or on adjoining properties which are within falling distance of your proposed development?   ○ Yes   ● No

Will any trees or hedges need to be removed or pruned in order to carry out your proposal?   ○ Yes   ● No

8. Parking

Will the proposed works affect existing car parking arrangements?   ○ Yes   ● No

9. Authority Employee/Member

With respect to the Authority, I am:
    (a) a member of staff
    (b) an elected member
    (c) related to a member of staff
    (d) related to an elected member

          Do any of these statements apply to you?   ○ Yes   ● No

10. Site Visit

Can the site be seen from a public road, public footpath, bridleway or other public land?   ● Yes   ○ No

If the planning authority needs to make an appointment to carry out a site visit, whom should they contact? (Please select only one)

○ The agent   ● The applicant   ○ Other person

11. Materials

Please state what materials (including type, colour and name) are to be used externally (if applicable):

Walls - description:
Description of *existing* materials and finishes:

Brick

Description of *proposed* materials and finishes:

Brick to match existing

Roof - description:
Description of *existing* materials and finishes:

Concrete tiles

Description of *proposed* materials and finishes:

Concrete tiles to match existing

Windows - description:
Description of *existing* materials and finishes:

Upvc

Description of *proposed* materials and finishes:

Upvc

Are you supplying additional information on submitted plan(s)/drawing(s)/design and access statement?   ● Yes   ○ No

If Yes, please state plan/drawing references for the plan(s)/drawing(s)/design and access statement:

Drawing 784/03

12. Certificates (Certificate A)

Certificate of Ownership - Certificate A
Town and Country Planning (Development Management Procedure) (England) Order 2010 Certificate under Article 12

I certify/The applicant certifies that on the day 21 days before the date of this application nobody except myself/the applicant was the owner (*owner is a person with a freehold interest or leasehold interest with at least 7 years left to run*) of any part of the land to which the application relates, and that none of the land to which the application relates is, or is part of, an agricultural holding ("*agricultural holding*" *has the meaning given by reference to the definition of "agricultural tenant" in section. 65(8) of the Act*)

Title: Mr   First name: Frank   Surname: Evans

Person role: Applicant   Declaration date: 30/06/2014   ☒ Declaration made

13. Declaration

I/we hereby apply for planning permission/consent as described in this form and the accompanying plans/drawings and additional information. I/we confirm that, to the best of my/our knowledge, any facts stated are true and accurate and any opinions given are the genuine opinions of the person(s) giving them.   ☒ Date 30/06/2014

Figure 6.1 (*Continued*)

APPLICANT'S NAME AND ADDRESS

The applicant does not have to be the owner as you can make an application on someone else's property, for example, where you are a prospective purchaser. If for some reason you do not wish to use your own name, an application can be made in another person's or company's name, as long as the correct notices are served (see below). Where an application site is owned by more than one person, you can choose between making the application in the name of all owners or making it in the name of one and sending a notice to the others. You are not obliged to give your own address and could instead give the address of a third party to receive correspondence on your behalf, such as your agent or a solicitor. There are companies which trawl planning applications and sell on names and addresses for marketing purposes. Whatever address you give might receive marketing material from contractors and building product suppliers.

AGENT'S NAME AND ADDRESS

Where you employ a professional to help you with a planning application, such as a planning consultant or designer, that person would normally complete the forms and enter his or her own name here. However, this need not be the case. You could get a designer to produce drawings or a planning consultant to write a planning statement for you, leaving you to fill in the forms and make the application. If an agent's name and address is given on the application form, the council will correspond with that person unless you ask them to do otherwise.

DESCRIPTION OF THE PROPOSAL

In this section you state what it is you are applying for permission to do. The development you are proposing should be described as concisely and precisely as possible, for example:

► erection of a dwelling

► erection of a two-storey rear extension

- conversion to a single dwelling
- conversion of loft space to accommodation with front dormer window
- erection of a garage
- formation of an access
- construction of a tennis court
- change of use from agricultural to domestic garden

It is not appropriate – or, necessarily, helpful – to describe your scheme in great detail or glowing terms, in order to sell it to the council or neighbours. Application drawings show the proposed work. An overly detailed description might make your scheme sound far more extensive than it is and scare neighbours into objecting. Notification letters and site notices state the description and, unless members of the public look up the application, this is the only indication they will see of the nature of the proposal. In the case of a new house, it is not necessary to specify a number of bedrooms, number of storeys, size or style. The council will, though, want the public to get an idea of what is proposed. So for extensions, it can be worth giving a broad indication of which part of the building is being extended. On receipt of an application, the council will consider the description given on the form and might amend it. Some councils are wordier than others.

Remember this

The description of the proposal on the form will define what you have permission to do.

If you make an outline planning application, there are boxes to tick to indicate which, if any, reserved matters or details are being applied for at this stage. Reserved matters are access, appearance, landscaping, layout and scale. You do not have to apply for any of these details. If you do include any of them, though, you need to supply sufficient information and drawings in the application for the council to be able to assess that aspect.

SITE ADDRESS

This is usually a straight-forward matter and you can enter the full address and postcode. It only needs thinking about where the property does not have its own postal address. This can be the case for vacant sites in built-up areas, parts of larger sites and areas of previously undeveloped land in the countryside. The location plan (see below) will identify the land precisely so all that is needed here is general description to say where the property is located. Some examples for situations where there is not a postal address are:

▶ land adjoining Apple Tree Cottage

▶ land between Coopers Mews and Bank Street

▶ site west of Harpers Yard

▶ land adjacent to 34 Green Lane

▶ plot between 37 and 41 Baker Close

▶ land north of Langley Avenue

PRE-APPLICATION ADVICE

Where you have spoken to a planning officer in advance, enter the name of the officer and quote any reference number that might have been given in correspondence. Pre-application consultation is not a requirement so ticking the 'no' box does not count against you. You are asked to give brief details of the 'advice' received. You can if you wish enter 'see attached letter' and deal with this in your planning letter/statement or say 'see planning officer's letter dated …' where the response was in writing. Otherwise, summarize what the planning officer said. There is nothing to be gained by grossly overstating any positive statements made or misrepresenting negative comments as the officer who deals with the application will check to see what was said.

ACCESS AND RIGHTS OF WAY

This section has tick boxes where you indicate whether the proposal involves new or altered vehicle or pedestrian access points. Unless you are making changes to an existing access or forming a new access, perhaps to relocate your drive or to serve a new dwelling, the answers are likely to be 'no'. Where a new access is to be formed, it will need to comply with highway standards (see Chapter 3). You are asked about diversions of rights of way. The grant of planning permission does not override any public or private right of way and it is sensible to investigate the scope for diversion or extinguishment of either before embarking on an application so as to avoid wasting time on a scheme you would not be able to implement.

WASTE STORAGE AND COLLECTION

This might seem like a trivial matter but some councils do get excited about bins. Many require new development to have bin enclosures with space for landfill and recyclables, depending on the waste collection regime of the council. This is not likely to cause problems except in tight urban sites where space outside the property is limited. Councils have departments which deal with waste and the officers there can tell you the requirements and can often suggest solutions where standard arrangements would not be possible.

MATERIALS

The form asks for the type, colour and name of existing and proposed external building materials. In many cases, the council attaches a condition to planning permissions requiring samples of materials to be approved or, sometimes, requiring external materials used to match the existing building. If you know the exact type of material you want to use, you can give the precise specification. Otherwise, it is usually sufficient to give a general description, such as 'brick', 'coloured render', 'tile' and 'timber'. Where the application is outline, it is quite likely you will not know the materials. Unless you opt to reserve all the details for later consideration, the online form insists something is entered in these boxes so you can just write 'reserved matter' or 'to be decided' to keep it happy.

PARKING

Proposals for extensions or alterations might well not affect existing parking arrangements. If an extension or outbuilding would be built on an area used for parking, you might need to replace the spaces elsewhere. Proposals for new dwellings – whether conversions, new build or subdivision – outside central urban areas are likely to need off-street parking. Councils have standards for parking provision and, where at all possible, your scheme should provide the spaces sought. In addition to car parking, new dwellings are expected to have cycle storage. This can be difficult for flats and some conversions in densely built-up areas. Various creative solutions exist for many such situations. The numbers of existing and proposed parking spaces are entered on the form where this is known.

FOUL SEWAGE

There are various options for drainage. The application form lists the options: mains sewer, septic tank, package treatment plant and cesspit. Most domestic properties are connected to the main sewer running in the road outside the property. It is in rural areas, not served by the mains, that houses have modern private treatment systems, septic tanks which treat the effluent, or cesspits which are sealed collection chambers requiring periodic emptying. For developments to existing houses, any relocated sinks, baths, showers or toilets will just connect back into whatever the present system is. Similarly, extensions will tap into the existing system. Where a new dwelling is concerned and there is no mains sewer to connect to, you need to ascertain how it would be drained.

FLOOD RISK

New dwellings proposed in areas identified as liable to flooding usually require justification and the submission of a flood risk assessment. You are asked whether the application site is within a flood risk area. You can find out whether your property is in such an area from the websites of the Environment Agency, Scottish Environment Protection Agency or Rivers Agency in Northern Ireland. The form also requires you to state what method of surface water (rain) drainage is proposed. For existing properties, the new building or use is likely to discharge into the existing system and you might need to investigate what that is. In most cases, soakaways on the site are used. These are holes excavated in the ground filled with rubble into which downpipes from gutters discharge. In built-up areas there might be a public surface water drain, similar to the foul drainage system, with which to connect. Where there is a pond or water course with capacity nearby, rain water might be channelled to them. Sustainable drainage systems are an alternative, more applicable to larger developments.

BIODIVERSITY AND GEOLOGY

The form asks about the presence of protected species, important habitats or geological features on or near the application site. Refer to the guidance notes to help you answer the questions. If there are natural features which might be affected by the proposal, a specialist survey and report would have to be carried out and submitted to the council.

EXISTING USE

While the form invites a description of the current use, a one-word answer is normally sufficient. Where the proposal concerns a house or flat or domestic garden, you can just enter 'residential'. You also have to state whether the site is vacant and, if so, what the last use had been. Usually the appropriate responses are clear. However, in some circumstances the answers to these questions need to be considered more carefully. It is generally better for the site to be in the intended use. For example, where part of garden is proposed to be, or has already been, divided off to become a plot for a new house, it is likely to be advantageous to describe it as 'residential'. It is generally better for the site to have some active use rather than be vacant. For example, where a new dwelling use is being justified wholly or partly on the basis of replacing some other existing use, it is likely to be advantageous to say the site is not vacant and enter the existing use. Obviously, you need to answer these and all the other questions on the form honestly and accurately.

TREES AND HEDGES

Where there are trees in the way of any proposed building or close enough that the tree could be affected, you might need to include a tree survey and report in your application. This is only likely to be the case where the tree is a good specimen and makes some positive contribution to the area. You can ask the council in advance whether a tree survey will be required – when carrying out pre-application consultation, for example – or submit your application and wait to see whether the council asks for one. The latter strategy could be risky, if the case officer does not decide a report is necessary until late on in the consideration of the application and is not prepared to let the application go beyond the target timescale, waiting for a report to be provided. Keep in mind that planning permission would only entitle you to fell trees necessary to carry out the development. Any other work would require separate consent, where the tree concerned is protected.

NON-RESIDENTIAL DEVELOPMENT

On non-householder application forms, there are several questions that relate to commercial and other types of development. Assuming your proposal is for a residential scheme of some kind, including domestic grounds and outbuildings, you can tick the 'no' box and leave the remainder blank.

SITE AREA

The figure you give should be the area of the application site which is edged with a red line on your location plan (see below).

For outline applications, the application fee paid to the council is calculated on the site area. The red line on the location plan only has to include the land where building and engineering works and any change of use is proposed. Consequently, when outline applications are made on sites of over 0.1 hectares, it can be expedient not to include the whole ownership within the application site in order to minimize the fee. If you are having drawings prepared by a designer, he or she should be able to advise you of the area of the site. Otherwise, it is a case of using a scale ruler and calculator to work it out. Where the fee is not calculated on site area, you do not need to be overly precise in the figure you give.

OWNERSHIP CERTIFICATES

Since you do not have to be the owner of the property, in respect of which you make a planning application, the applicant (or the agent) has to complete an ownership certificate and inform any site owner(s), other than the applicant, that an application is being made. You also have to say whether any of the land is subject to an agricultural tenancy, even when the site is in the middle of a built-up area.

There are four possible certificates:

▶ The applicant is the only owner and there are no agricultural tenants (certificate A).

▶ The applicant is not the only owner and/or there is an agricultural tenant (certificate B).

▶ The applicant is not the only owner and/or there is an agricultural tenant, some of whom are not known (certificate C).

▶ The applicant is not the only owner and/or there is an agricultural tenant, none of which are known (certificate D).

In most cases, the applicant is the owner of all the land involved and there is no agricultural tenant, so the first of these certificates is the appropriate one. If you are making an application, perhaps to establish that planning permission will be given before buying a property, and do not yet own the site concerned, certificate B has to be signed. Where a property is owned by a number of people and the application is not made in the name of all of them, the same certificate is used. It is ownership of the area of land identified as the planning application site which is important. So, for example, should you not own some or all of the access drive from your property to the public road, you would include the entire drive in your application site and, again, complete certificate B. When signing such a certificate, you have to give the name and address of the owner or other owners and send them a notice about the application. There is a standard form for this on which you enter the site address, your name, the description of the proposal as set out in the application form, and the address of the council.

That is all quite straightforward when you know who, apart from you, owns the land. It is not that uncommon, however, to come across areas of land whose ownership is not clear. In these circumstances, either certificate C or D must be filled in, depending on whether you know the identity of any of the other owners. You are required to state what steps have been taken to find out who owns the land, such as Land Registry searches. Such applications have to be advertised in the public notices section of a local newspaper. The council will be able to tell you which papers are appropriate for the location of the site. There is a standard wording to use, similar to the notice for serving on known owners, which you get from the council or online. You need to contact one of the designated newspapers and arrange to place (and pay for) the advert. Staff members at these papers are generally familiar with publishing such notices and the process is not complicated.

Drawings

The types and number of drawings you need to submit with your application vary according to the nature of the proposal and the type of application. The council's application guidance and validation checklists set out what is required but it is as well to speak to an officer in the planning department to make sure that, in the particular circumstances of your project, all the drawings required are supplied and that you do not waste time and money on preparing unnecessary drawings. For example, where an application is for the change of use of a building which would not be altered or is a retrospective application for minor works, councils sometimes accept photos instead of drawings. For all but the simplest applications, you are better off getting a professional to produce drawings for you. Even so, it is advisable to understand the requirements to help you give the appropriate instructions and appreciate the implications of what is prepared for you.

All application drawings should be to an identified metric scale. It is highly desirable to give them a reference number with each revision marked with a new letter, for example, 'revision A'. For more complex schemes, such as designing a new house, there can be many versions of the drawings and clear labelling helps to avoid confusion.

Remember this

Get building drawings prepared by a professional.

LOCATION PLAN

This is based on an up-to-date Ordnance Survey map, typically at a scale of 1:1,250 (see Figure 6.2). Usually A4-sized paper is sufficient, although for a larger site it could go onto A3 paper. You can buy Ordnance Survey map extracts from the council and various retailers, including online, as paper or electronic copies. The plan needs to show the scale, a north point and sufficient roads and buildings to make the location clear. The boundaries of the application site have to be edged with a red line which can be drawn on to a paper plan in felt pen or added to an electronic version using the appropriate software. The defined site should include all land on which new building or work would take place as well as all land where the use would change. This would include the access to the property from a public road, visibility splays at the access

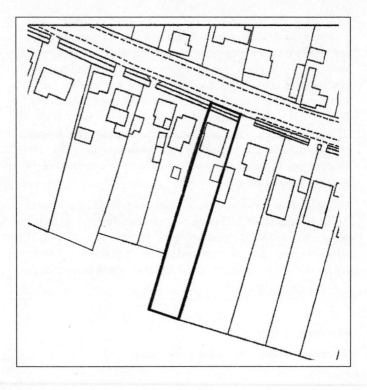

Figure 6.2 Sample location plan

point, areas to be landscaped, parking and turning areas, and the area of land to be used in conjunction with the building. Any other land owned by the applicant adjoining or near the application site is edged in a blue line. What land to include in an application site is usually obvious. As mentioned above, since council fees for outline applications are based on the application site area, this might influence what you choose to define as the application site.

BLOCK PLAN
Sometimes called a site plan, this is a drawing showing the proposal in relation to what is around it, often drawn at 1:500 scale (see Figure 6.3). The scale should be specified and a north

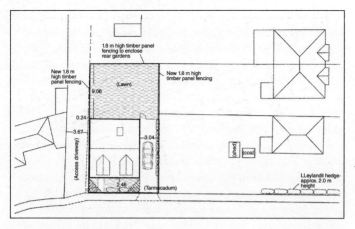

Figure 6.3 Sample block plan

point included. Any new buildings and all existing buildings should be shown with dimensions to boundaries from proposed buildings stated on the drawing. Depending on the nature of the scheme, a block plan would also include:

- roads, accesses and footpaths nearby

- public rights of way on and next to the site

- the position of trees on the site and on adjoining land

- hard-surfaced areas

- proposed walls or fencing

If you make an outline application and are not seeking approval of the layout at that stage, ensure any new buildings shown on the plan are marked as being illustrative.

SITE PLAN

While different councils and professionals call drawings different names, 'site plan' or 'site layout plan' is often used to describe a larger-scale version of a block plan. The larger scale, typically 1:200, enables these drawings to show the proposed layout in greater detail, for example the extent of tree canopies, different surfaced and planted areas, access arrangements and existing features of the site.

ELEVATIONS

Elevations are the front, back and sides of the building (see Figure 6.4). For new buildings, the drawings would show the complete design of the structure including all windows and doors and where different materials would be used, such as brick, render and tile hanging. Councils sometimes ask for materials to be specified on the drawings. It is usually best to give a fairly general description to allow yourself latitude in case a particular type of material is not available or you change your mind about a colour. Elevations are often drawn to a scale of 1:100 or 1:50. If the proposed building would be close to an existing building, a neighbouring house for example, it is helpful to show the adjoining property. Where the proposal is to alter a building, unless the changes are very minor, your drawings need to show the building as it exists and as it would be after the works.

While most application drawings can be presented in quite a plain way, it is the elevations that really show how the property will appear. Consequently, it is worth commissioning elevation drawings that look attractive. Most drawings are done on computer rather than being hand drawn and they can look stark. Having said that, computer aided design programmes are now sophisticated, allowing shading and other refinements to help bring a design to life. If appearance is critical, perhaps a property in a Conservation Area or next to a listed building, you could consider getting hand drawn elevations from someone with artistic flair to help sell the scheme. Including existing trees, hedges and shrubs behind, around and, in outline, in front of the building softens its appearance and shows how it would blend into the setting. It is sometimes a good idea to show the outline of properties beyond the application building, to demonstrate similar height or bulk, or the outline of previous application schemes to show how the revised proposal compares.

Remember this

Your project has to be built in accordance with the approved application drawings.

FLOOR PLANS

These show the layout of each level of the building which would be used (see Figure 6.5), including basement and loft space where accommodation would be provided there. Generally, the council is not likely to be overly concerned with the internal arrangement of the accommodation itself. It can, though, be relevant for assessing overlooking, outlook and daylight. Some councils have minimum space standards and will use floor plans for working out whether the proposal complies.

ROOF PLAN

This is a plan view of the roof which is helpful for clarifying the structure and look of the roof, as this is not always clear from the elevation drawings. It would show ridges, hips, dormers and flat roof sections.

CONTEXT DRAWINGS AND OTHER REPRESENTATIONS

Such drawings can be scale drawings, perhaps showing two or three properties either side of the proposed building. These are often referred to as a 'street scene' and give an impression of how the development would look in context. While these can be useful, they do not actually convey what the view would be because such drawings do not take into account perspective. For this reason, where design and impact in the setting is an important factor, consider getting perspective drawings prepared. These would not be to scale and should be labelled 'illustrative'. Computer programmes can produce these images derived from the standard technical drawings.

There is also 3D visualization software which can place a representation of the building into photographs taken from various vantage points. The old fashioned alternative is an artist's impression, which often results in the most attractive image. A computer generated representation of the proposed building can look false and runs the risk that it would stand out or not fit well in its setting. Review any illustrative drawings critically prior to submitting them to make sure they are accurate and actually present a favourable impression. Producing them will have cost you money but if they are not going to sell the scheme, it is better not to use them.

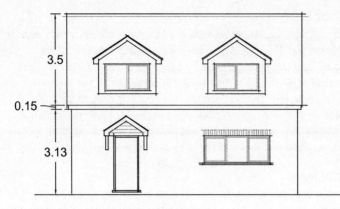

FRONT ELEVATION

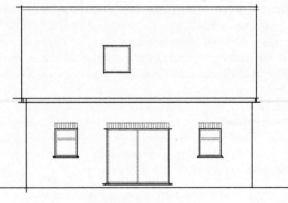

REAR ELEVATION

Figure 6.4 Sample elevations (drawings courtesy of Woolhampton Design Centre)

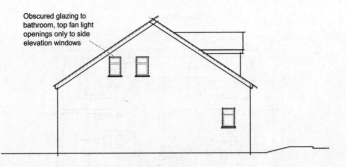

Obscured glazing to bathroom, top fan light openings only to side elevation windows

L.H. SIDE ELEVATION

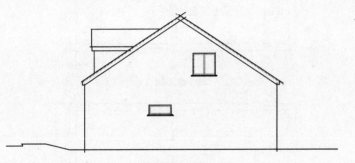

R.H. SIDE ELEVATION

Figure 6.4 (*Continued*)

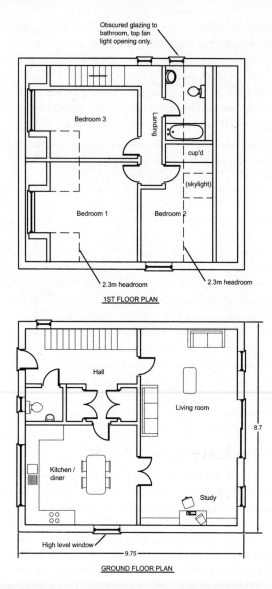

Obscured glazing to bathroom, top fan light opening only.

Bedroom 3

Landing

cup'd

(skylight)

Bedroom 1

Bedroom 2

2.3m headroom

2.3m headroom

1ST FLOOR PLAN

Hall

Living room

8.7

Kitchen / diner

Study

High level window

9.75

GROUND FLOOR PLAN

Figure 6.5 Sample floor plans (drawings courtesy of Woolhampton Design Centre)

Where there is sufficient at stake and the building is relatively complex, you can get a model made so planning officers, councillors and, maybe, members of the public can get a full three-dimensional impression. The model might be not only of the building but could include the surrounding site, to show how the building would appear in relation to the land levels and contours, as well as to other nearby structures.

Design and access statement

A design and access statement is a statutory requirement with certain applications. The circumstances in which one must be submitted and its content differ between UK countries. Generally speaking, design and access statements are applicable to large-scale development but can be required for single new dwellings. The council's application guidance or planning department staff should be able to advise you whether one is applicable. A design and access statement is an explanation of the design principles adopted, how the design responds to the context and how the scheme makes provision for vehicular access and movement of people around the development. Where required for small-scale proposals, these statements can be fairly simple. Designers often prepare design and access statements to accompany their drawings and sometimes veer towards producing a greater volume of written material than is really necessary.

Planning letter/statement

Even where it is not a requirement, it is desirable to submit some sort of supporting material in writing. Where a design and access statement has to be submitted, that might be all that is needed (see above). Alternatively, you can combine a planning statement with a design and access statement in one document. If you do that, mention both in the title so the council knows you are submitting everything that is required. For minor works, a short letter can suffice. Such a basic statement should, at least, describe the proposed work to make it easy for the planning officer to understand what it is about when he or she is studying the drawings. It could explain how it fits with existing buildings and the site and would not cause problems for neighbours. For larger-scale, more complex or potentially controversial schemes, or where the planning officer might not support the proposal, a full statement is advisable. There is no set formula for a planning statement but comprehensive ones tend to have fairly standard headings. A typical statement would be set out as follows:

- Introduction

- Location and site description

- Proposed development

- Planning history of the site and planning permissions on other sites

- Planning policies relevant to the application

- Assessment – the case for the development in light of the preceding factors

- Conclusion

The appropriate level of detail will vary in each case but the fewer the words, the more likely it is they will be read and digested. You can take a cue on what to include and how much detail to give from planning officers' reports on similar applications.

Remember this

Put forward a case in favour of your proposal in a letter or statement.

INTRODUCTION

This can simply say that the statement relates to the planning application, give the address and set out what the application is for (i.e. the description given on the form). If any other clarification is required, for example that it is a revised proposal after a previous application, it can go in here too.

LOCATION AND SITE DESCRIPTION

The location can be stated quite simply because the officers will know the area and the site is shown on the location plan. If the site is difficult to find or is part of a larger property, you can add a little more detail.

The description typically covers the shape, area and topography of the site, what is on the site, including trees and other vegetation, and the boundaries. The nature of any existing buildings can be outlined. Concentrate on points that influenced the design of the scheme or which affect its impact, for example on neighbours, the wider area or views.

Go on to describe adjoining properties and their relevant features, such as the position of windows, design or distances to boundaries. You can also sum up the nature of the area, for example, 'residential estate of semi-detached post-war houses' or 'detached houses set in spacious plots'. If there are similar developments in the area, state this and give addresses because they will be part of the physical character of the area.

PROPOSED DEVELOPMENT

If you submit a separate design and access statement, a description of the scheme will probably be in there and there is no need to duplicate the information. Otherwise, include a brief outline of what is proposed. The building and/or alterations you want to carry out are all in the drawings so it is not necessary to go into every last detail. Concentrate on the main features, such as size, layout, distances to boundaries and other buildings, style and materials, window positions, landscaping, and access and parking arrangements.

PLANNING HISTORY

Previous planning decisions – whether permissions or refusals – and what was said during the course of the assessments can be relevant to a subsequent proposal. You do not need to mention every previous application, only those that you think have some relevance to the current proposal. For instance, if a similar scheme has been approved and could still be built, that would be a material consideration. In refusing a previous planning application it might have been clear that, with certain changes, perhaps a reduction in ridge height or width, the scheme would have been acceptable. The planning officers' reports are likely to be key planning history documents but there could be others, such as highway authority responses or minutes of committee meetings, which contain helpful comments. Quote the reference numbers of any applications to which you refer and point out the pertinent aspects, quoting sections of relevant text.

In the same way, you can refer to decisions on other sites in support of your case. Keep in mind that planning does not work on the basis of precedents (see Chapter 3), yet other cases may contain points of principle you can use, for example how a planning policy has been interpreted.

PLANNING POLICIES

As set out in Chapter 3, planning policies are the starting point for assessing planning applications. It is highly desirable that your statement explains how or the extent to which the proposed development complies with planning policies. Make sure you identify which are the most applicable national and local policies and guidance. If you have not carried out a pre-application consultation, you can find this information by speaking to a planning policy officer, looking up the policy documents yourself, or both. Planning officers might not refer to, or might place less emphasis on, national policies, often preferring their own council's policies and, generally speaking, for smaller-scale projects, local polices are likely to be most relevant. You can always ask about national policies specifically or look up them up yourself. Quote policy references and paragraph numbers in the statement and, if you wish, go a step further and summarize the main requirements of each relevant policy and guideline.

ASSESSMENT

In this section, bring everything together. Up to this point, you should have said what the proposal is, what the circumstances are and what main planning policies apply. Now you say how your proposal measures up.

You could start with assessing the scheme against planning policy. Study the policies and say in what ways your scheme is consistent with their terms. Where policies list various criteria, explain how it meets all the relevant ones. The planning officers should be familiar with the policy documents and have them to hand so there is no need to include the whole policy in your statement. However, it is often worth quoting short passages to help make a point.

Then you can go on to deal with material considerations (see Chapter 3). Here you can make points such as how the planning history or decisions on other similar proposals indicate permission should be given in your case. Also, go through any relevant considerations not already covered by planning policies and guidance, for example design, site layout, visual impact, effect on neighbours, access and parking and so on. Explain how the development would not cause harm to any of these interests. If your proposal would be partly, or even completely against any planning policy, say why the particular circumstances (from a planning rather than a personal perspective) of the proposal make it acceptable. An example could be that a house, proposed in an area where planning policy says new dwellings will not be permitted, would replace an unsightly building used for industrial purposes which causes disturbance.

CONCLUSION
Sum up the key points and say, where you can, that your proposal complies with all relevant national and local planning policy.

Specialists' reports
Examples of the sort of additional information which can be required with planning applications are given in Chapter 4. The most common ones are tree survey, highway report, heritage statement and ecological survey, especially bats, owls and newts. Some information sought might be very basic and within the ability of your consultant to deal with. Where the council or your consultant tells you specialist input is needed, you will need to commission an appropriate assessment and report for submission. If you are using a professional to help you with the application, that person can probably recommend someone with whom he or she has worked before. Councils are usually reluctant to recommend professionals but can sometimes be persuaded to say who has carried out similar work on other applications. You can

also look up other applications for proposals similar to yours in the same area and see who those applicants used. Failing that, search online, contact the appropriate professional body or look in phone or business directories.

It is worth establishing with the planning department what level of detail is required. It might be that the council is concerned about one particular tree, not every tree on the site, or would prefer to receive a one or two page letter, rather than a bound report with numerous technical appendices. Consultants can have a tendency towards leaving no stone unturned in their investigations, without regard to time or cost. They also have a vested interest in finding something on the site that requires further investigation or subsequent monitoring. Try to find a specialist who is practical, who looks for solutions rather than problems and who appreciates that his or her work is costing you money you would rather be spending on the project. Look for individuals and practices of the right scale for the job. Sole traders and small firms are likely to be appropriate and affordable for schemes involving single dwellings, as opposed to large national or international companies. Specialists' reports can be expensive so it is worth getting two or three quotes.

Timing can be an issue. Some wildlife surveys can only be undertaken at certain times of year or the existence of contamination can require monitoring over a period. Provided you are aware of the need for the report in advance, you can commission it in good time or delay submission of the application. If the need only becomes apparent after submission, you will need to act quickly or consider withdrawing the application while the work is done.

Application fee

There is a fee to pay the council for making a planning application. Payment has to be made when the application is submitted. There are scales of fees which are set separately in the UK countries. Fees for full applications are based on the number of dwellings to be built. At the time of writing, these are around £330–£390 for each dwelling and about half that for work on a house, such as extensions and garden buildings, with fees in Northern Ireland being slightly higher. Outline application fees are based on the area of the application site with the same fee as a dwelling being charged for each 0.1ha, except in Northern Ireland where it is about half the dwelling rate for each 0.1ha. Your council should have a schedule of fees on its website and at its offices. The Planning Portal website has a fee calculator. Fees for most domestic planning applications are quite straightforward. Fees for some of the other types of application in England might be less well publicized. If in any doubt, speak to the planning department.

There are some fee exemptions. In particular, an applicant is entitled to one free application where an application is made on the same site, for the same type of development within 12 months of the previous decision. This covers situations where a revised proposal is submitted after a refusal, approval or withdrawal.

There are various ways to pay planning application fees. You can post or deliver a cheque to the council. If doing this, write the application reference number on the back and, where you are not making the application on paper, attach a covering letter. Some councils accept online card payment via the Planning Portal or ePlanning Scotland. When completing the application online, if your council accepts that method, the option will be presented when you get to the final stage of submission. Alternatively, some councils allow you to make card payments over the phone. Once the application has been sent, phone the council during office hours to do the transaction.

Covering letter

A covering letter is not a requirement but is useful nonetheless. It need do no more than record everything you are submitting as part of the application. Write the full property address of the application site clearly and prominently on the letter as a heading. Say the letter is accompanying a planning application and what that application is for. List the numbers of the drawings, making it clear which, if any, are illustrative, all the supporting documents and the amount and method of payment. The covering letter can serve as a checklist for you and the council, and allows you to confirm what was submitted should you need to do this at some point after submission, perhaps a couple of years later when the detail of the application might not still be clear in your mind. If it transpires you make a number of applications, this will be especially helpful.

If your supporting letter/statement is relatively short, you can combine it with the covering letter.

Legal agreements and the Community Infrastructure Levy (CIL)

The nature of these is explained in Chapter 4. Your pre-application investigations and consultations should identify when a legal agreement is likely to be needed. It is as well to be prepared for this before submitting your application. Councils deal with the process of getting legal agreements in place in different ways. Speak to the planning officers to ascertain how your council manages this. Many councils are sufficiently focused on meeting target dates for deciding applications that they will not delay making a decision while a legal agreement is drawn up. In such cases, they would rather turn down an application on the basis that a required agreement has not been provided. This is complicated by the need to get a mortgagee to sign the document, where there is a mortgage on the property. If necessary, get the document prepared in advance and submit it with your application. That might be possible where the council's requirements are known at the outset. However, some councils do not calculate financial contributions precisely until an application is submitted. In cases of legal agreements required for reasons other than financial contributions, the need might not be identified until the application is made. Many councils produce standard forms or templates for legal agreements. Since it is a legally binding document affecting your property, it is sensible to get a solicitor to check it before you sign it.

Where councils have their CIL regimes in place, there will be a simple form you need to complete as part of the application. This asks about the nature of the application and floor areas in order to work out whether the project is liable to CIL and, if so, what the payment will be. For outline permissions, the liability is assessed when the details of the development are approved. The CIL form has to be submitted along with the remainder of the application documents.

Focus points

* Decide whether to make your application online or on paper.
* Obtain and complete the correct forms, referring to the guidance notes.
* Commission the necessary drawings.
* Prepare a supporting letter/statement.
* Find out whether any other documents are required and get them prepared.
* Submit your application to the council with the correct fee.

Next step

Your application has now been submitted. However, this should not be the end of the process if you wish to maximize your chances of getting planning permission. It is desirable to monitor the progress of the application and get involved if queries or problems arise.

Managing your application

In this chapter you will learn:

- ▶ *Why it is worthwhile monitoring the progress of your application*
- ▶ *The importance of liaising with the case officer*
- ▶ *When and how to contact councillors and consultees*
- ▶ *How to deal with objections*
- ▶ *What happens at planning committee meetings*

Validation and acknowledgement

On receipt of an application, administrative staff in the planning department will check it to ensure the necessary forms have been completed fully and all the required drawings and documents and the correct application fee have been submitted (see Chapter 4). Provided they believe your application is all present and correct, they will send an acknowledgement letter. Should they think that some essential aspect is missing from an application or something needs clarification or is incorrect, they will write to the person who made the application, which will be your agent, if there is one. Efficient councils will email their responses promptly or may even phone if they have relatively simple queries. Less efficient ones can take a while to respond and then send a letter which can take a week or so to generate as it churns through the council's system.

Until such time as the application has been validated, it is not officially made and the timetables and assessment process do not begin. Therefore, in order to hasten a decision, it is desirable to get your application validated as soon as possible. Once registered, the application will be posted on the council's website (see below). If nothing appears and you do not hear from the council within, say, a week of submission, phone the planning department and ask to speak to an officer who deals with validating planning applications. Ask about your application giving the property address and reference where the application was submitted online. By this means, you can make sure the application has been received and is in the system and whether there is anything outstanding. You might find the council has a backlog of applications awaiting validation and yours is in the pile with the others. In that circumstance, the officer should, at least, be able to give an indication of how long validation is taking and you can make a diary note to call back. You could be informed the council is about to write saying the application is not considered valid and be able to ascertain the outstanding matters.

On receipt of an acknowledgement letter, note the application reference which you should use in any subsequent correspondence with the council and, where such information is given, the name and direct dial phone number and email address of the case officer. Councils sometimes change the description of the application. Where that happens, make sure the council's description still accurately reflects the proposal and contact the case officer if you do not agree with it. The letter should give the date of validation, normally the day after receipt of all the necessary documentation and fee. Some specify the target date for a decision but if not, you can always calculate it yourself and make a note of it.

Where the council indicates your application is not valid, the letter itemises the questions, errors or additional material considered necessary. Read this carefully. Often a phone call to the officer named in the letter is worthwhile to go over the points. It is not unusual to find the officers have not fully understood what has been submitted and that the information sought has been provided or is not relevant. Otherwise, you can clarify exactly what the council wants, including the level of detail.

While councils are not supposed to ask for a document just because it is included on a list of local validation requirements, some still do. Only that material which is necessary, in the circumstances of each case, in order to assess a proposal should be requested. Local authorities are, though, risk-averse and so will, on occasion, ask for a report or statement on a matter – such as a tree report or ecological survey – rather than risk facing criticism should it emerge, during or after the consideration of an application, that a development caused harm. It costs the council nothing to request this information. If the officers cannot be persuaded to drop a request for additional material, you can organize its provision (see Chapter 6) or, in England, challenge the council's request (see Chapter 4).

Monitoring your application online

Councils have different systems on their websites recording the progress of planning applications. The best ones include all documents sent to and by the council in connection with the application, which is as good as seeing the council's file at its offices. Others just display the submitted application documents. Documents are usually posted on the council's website within a few days to a week after receipt. So, if you have access to the internet, this is a good way to stay in touch with the progress of your application.

Typing the council's name into a search engine often results in a link straight to the council's application search facility, as it is a popular search. Failing that, many councils have a link prominent on their home page. Otherwise, there will be a list of services or departments and by clicking through a few levels, you should find the application search or comment page. Having found the application page, you can usually enter your property address or the application reference number, shown in the acknowledgement letter, in a search box to access your application.

The information available about applications varies. The most comprehensive sites show the name and contacts for the case officer, dates for validation, consultation periods, target date for a decision and a committee meeting (where appropriate), and whether the application is likely to be delegated or go to committee. On most sites there is a tab for application documents you can click on. There you should be able to see all the documents you sent to the council and, should you send additional material after submission, they should appear within a few days too. Good sites also show consultation responses as they are received, any correspondence with the council, objections and support from members of the public, site visit notes made by the planning officer and, when produced at the end of the assessment, the planning officer's report on the application and the decision notice.

Your application might be uploaded to the council's website even before you receive the acknowledgement letter so, as mentioned above, you can check whether the application is valid by monitoring the website in the days after submission. After validation, you can look up your application online as frequently as you wish, to see what appears. In terms of efficient monitoring, unless you are expecting something specific to be added, checking the site once a week is usually sufficient. Apart from following progress, the things to look for are adverse comments or questions arising which you might be able to address. You will find these in consultees' comments and objections, so check each of these documents when they appear.

Where an application is to be decided by planning committee, the officer's report might be uploaded to the application file on the website when it is made public before the meeting. Some councils do not do this but the report should still be available in the section of the council's website that deals with council meetings. Here it will show a timetable of all council committee meetings and agendas and minutes for these meetings. Search this section to locate the agenda for the relevant planning committee meeting and the officer's report on your application should be there.

Liaising with the case officer

The planning officer assigned to deal with your application (often referred to as the case officer) is instrumental in the eventual outcome of your application and will manage the council's assessment of it. Clearly this is a key person with whom to liaise in an effort to ensure a smooth passage and successful result. If the name of the officer is not on the acknowledgement letter or the website, phone the planning department to ask who it is. For uncontentious applications, the amount of contact necessary might be minimal. Where there are objections or complications, communication with the case officer can head off a refusal. You will need to strike a balance in your communications between staying in touch and not becoming a nuisance and risking alienating the officer. Bear in mind, your application will be just one of many of the officer's workload. Planning officers come in various personality types from cheerful and helpful to officious or inefficient. There are different levels of seniority from trainees to team leaders. Small-scale residential applications are more likely to be dealt with by more junior officers. When making contact, endeavour to get a sense of who you are dealing with. Arguing with or criticizing an officer is unlikely to dispose him or her to you favourably so always be courteous in your communications.

You can contact the officer by email but this might not be answered quickly and you will not get such a good sense of the person with whom you are dealing. Some councils have barriers in place to stop members of the public speaking directly and immediately to planning officers. There might be a call-back system whereby you leave a message and the officer is supposed to phone you within a specified time, perhaps one or two working days. Having spoken to the case officer once, you could decide whether to phone or email for subsequent communication.

Try phoning the case officer a week or two after you receive the acknowledgement letter. Councils have different ways of assessing applications but, at this early stage, the chances are that the case officer will scarcely be aware of your application and is unlikely to have looked at it in any detail. The purpose of an early call is to open the lines of communication, ascertain whether the officer has any initial questions and find out when would be an appropriate time to call back to see how the application is going. Some officers might say there is no need to contact them and they will contact you, if necessary. Otherwise, make a note in your diary to make contact again when the officer suggests.

If you are monitoring your application on the council's website, should anything significant arise, you could contact the case officer at that point. It would not be appropriate, though, to contact the officer in response to every comment made. If there are several objections, it would be better to wait until the end of the consultation period and then take action (see below).

Where the officer suggests a time to call back, phone again then. Alternatively, after the end of the consultation period is a good time to make contact. If you are monitoring the council's website, you should be able to see what has been said and can discuss any matters arising and ask what, if anything, you can usefully do in response. If you are not checking the website regularly, the case officer can tell you what comments have been received. Finish any conversation with the officer by asking when it would be appropriate to call again.

The case officer will visit the property and this provides an opportunity to meet and discuss the proposal. Quite often, officers turn up unannounced. However, if the officer needs to get into the site or house and no one is likely to be at the property during office hours, you can contact them to arrange a time for an inspection. The officer might be non-committal and, depending at what point in the process the visit is made, might not have received responses to consultation and publicity or considered the application. You can, though, discuss anything that has arisen and explain the proposal in person.

For applications going to committee for decision, obtain and read carefully the officer's report. It is not unknown for reports to contain factual mistakes. Should there be any which could be detrimental to your application, contact the officer to point them out. A line by line analysis of the report is not likely to achieve much and the officer will probably not change any opinions stated just because you disagree with them. The officer should double-check any factual points you question and, if found to be incorrect, should draw them to the attention of councillors in an addendum to the committee agenda or verbally at the meeting.

Contacting consultees

You can contact individuals and organizations who will be consulted by the council on your proposal before making a planning application. A planning officer should be able to tell you who would be consulted on the type of project you have in mind. Consultees fall into two categories, which can be thought of as non-technical and technical (see Chapter 4). Non-technical consultees include the parish council and, sometimes, local interest groups. However, in most cases it is not appropriate to speak to consultees before making an application. Exceptions for technical consultees might be where the application involves creating one or more dwellings and the site is in a flood risk area, where an access would be created and safety could be an issue, or significant works to a listed building.

Planning applications are normally considered by the parish council at one of its regular meetings. Consultees are supposed to respond to the council within three weeks so your application is likely to be considered early in the assessment process. Most parish councils allow applicants to speak at their meetings but, unless you suspect your application is likely to be controversial (which is not always easy to predict), there is probably no need to do so. If you want to speak at the meeting or just to attend and listen, contact the parish council clerk as soon as the application is submitted to find out at when it is likely to be considered and make the arrangements for speaking, if appropriate.

In the absence of any particular circumstances necessitating early contact, you can leave contacting technical consultees until such time as you discover that a consultee has made an adverse comment, recommended an unacceptable condition or raised a question. Through monitoring the application, you should be alerted to such a comment or question. In the first instance, try speaking to the case officer to gauge whether he or she thinks the response could be fatal to the application and whether they believe it would be advantageous to deal with the matter before a decision is made. The consultee's response will normally bear their name and, often, their contact details. Phone the consultee to discuss the point of concern and ascertain whether you can clarify any points or provide additional information that might satisfy them, such as another drawing or some technical specification, or maybe an email confirming some aspect of the scheme in more detail. Where that is possible, supply the information as quickly as possible. Follow this up to see whether it overcomes the consultee's concern and, if it does, urge them to write again to the planning officer indicating acceptance. You can then check this has been done on the council's website or by speaking to the case officer. Ultimately, the important point is that the case officer is happy with the proposal in light of whatever the consultee says.

Key idea

Consultees' comments can be included as conditions to your planning permission.

Neighbour support

As described in Chapter 5, you can get letters of support from neighbours in advance and submit them with your application. This is not a requirement, however, and you can wait until after the application has been made to enlist the backing of people in the vicinity. If you took the desirable step of informing neighbours about your proposals before finalizing the application, you can now advise them that the application has been submitted. It is likely that the council will write to them in any event, notifying them that an application has been submitted and inviting them to comment, if they wish.

Objections can cause problems for applications. Support is helpful. Silence is all right. Support can also help to offset objections. While the planning officer will form his or her own view, public comment can influence that and can certainly have an impact on councillors. Objections can cause councillors to call applications into committee for a decision and lead them to speak against those applications, sometimes overturning a favourable officer recommendation. So, your objective is to get as much support as you can, within reason, as you need to be proportionate. If your application is for a small rear extension, getting support from the immediately adjoining neighbours should be adequate. If your application is for a new house, and you know some people have concerns about it, getting support from a little way up and down the road could be worthwhile.

Comments can be made in a letter, email or via a comment form on the council's website. Despite their best intentions, people can be slow to put pen to paper or finger to keyboard. You can increase the chances of turning passive support into active support by offering to help. For example, you could collect neighbours' letters and send them to the council, provide stamped addressed envelopes, or draft letters, based on what the neighbours have said, for them to sign and again send these on to the council. You can provide computer literate neighbours with the appropriate council email address and application reference, or a link to the web page on the council's website for making online comments.

Contacting councillors

As noted in Chapter 5, for most applications it is not necessary to contact district councillors. The circumstances in which it can be appropriate to contact councillors include where:

▶ The planning officer has indicated he or she is unlikely to support your application.

▶ The application is attracting significant objection.

▶ You know objectors are speaking to councillors.

▶ Your application is going to committee with a recommendation for refusal.

Before attempting to make contact, check the council's policy on lobbying. There will be a council department which looks after councillors and committees and you can phone an officer there to ascertain the etiquette at your council. Despite councillors being elected, in theory, to represent constituents, you might find that no contact is allowed. At the other end of the spectrum, some councils do not seek to restrict access to councillors and there will be variations between these points. Councillors' postal and email addresses and, perhaps, phone numbers will be on the council's website.

In most instances where contact would be appropriate, it is best to contact the two or three councillors who represent the area where the property is located. You can also contact the chairman of the relevant planning committee, perhaps copying any written communication to him or her. You can also find out from the council which councillors are on the planning committee that may decide your application. While these would be prime targets for contact, you can still get in touch with others who might potentially be able to help more since they would not be involved in making the decision.

If the planning officer opposes your application, make contact with the councillors soon after the submitted application is acknowledged. Your first objective here is to get the application called into committee, otherwise it will probably just be refused by the officers as a delegated decision. Many councils have a limited period within which councillors can make a request for an application to go to committee. Where you know your application is definitely to be decided by the planning committee, you can wait until the officer's report is made public before deciding whether to get in touch with councillors. If your application is recommended for approval, in the absence of significant objection, you could let it be. If it is recommended for refusal, approach councillors then.

Key idea

Ultimately, it is the councillors who have the power to decide your application.

You will have to judge the nature of the first contact, partly based on what the officer says about speaking to councillors. It may be that an email or letter is appropriate, giving the property address, description of the proposed development and application reference, perhaps setting out the main points in favour of the scheme or countering the objections of neighbours or officers, and inviting the councillor to look into the application, speak to you or visit the site. Where you would like the application to be called in to committee, make the request and give the councillor reasons why that would be justified, such as the peculiar circumstances, point of principle to establish, or the level of local interest or support. Remember, the councillor could be a busy person and might have a great deal of council business to deal with already, so keep communication short and directly to the point. It may be that a phone call is appropriate for first contact. Be ready with the same sort of information that you might include in an email/letter.

The reaction you will get is unpredictable. Some councillors will brush you off and not wish to get involved. Some could acknowledge your approach and undertake to bear your views in mind. Others might visit the property to gauge the matters in dispute for themselves. Councillors who sit on the planning committee are often and understandably reluctant to meet applicants without officers present in order to avoid any appearance of impropriety. Councillors on the committee are also unlikely to express an opinion on how they will vote in the interests of being seen to remain open-minded in advance of the meeting. The councillor might suggest who else to speak to or action to take. Follow these up if they seem to be helpful. Mention to the councillors if you plan to attend the committee meeting so they know you will hear what they say – not, of course, that this will guarantee they support you.

Dealing with objections

Objections might be raised by:

- the case officer

- consultees

- neighbours/members of the public

- councillors

Whether and how to respond depends on how significant the objections appear to be. You can discuss any concerns of the case officer with him or her and the officer might suggest information you could usefully provide. For example, if a good specimen tree might be affected by your proposed works, the officer might suggest getting a report from a tree consultant or, if it is possible there are bats in the roof space, an inspection and report by a bat expert could settle the matter. It might just be a question of your writing to the council to clarify some aspect of the proposal.

Not every objection raised by the case officer is capable of being overcome. If the officer does not support the principle of the development, perhaps because it is in an area where the council does not favour granting permission, such as new houses outside built-up areas, there might be nothing that would change his or her mind. In that sort of situation, you could, nevertheless, look for examples of where similar schemes have been approved and draw these to the attention of the officer. Where the officer's concerns relate to planning policy or guidance, get details from the officer and look those up in the relevant document. See what they say and consider whether your proposal meets the terms and criteria. The applicability and interpretation of much planning policy is dependent on subjective judgements and there will not be a right or wrong view. You can look for other policies or guidance, such as government guidance, which might be put forward to counter any conflict with the policies mentioned. If you can come up with an answer to the officer's concern, write to the council setting this out. Planning policy can be technical and not readily accessible so, if you are uncertain about it, think about enlisting the help of a planning consultant.

Remember this

Where necessary, take action to overcome any concerns or objections while your application is being considered.

The case officer might raise points about the design or layout of the development. These could be choice of external materials, roof height or bulk, size of building, window positions, proximity to boundaries and many others. In that case, consider what is being said and see whether alterations could be made which would overcome or alleviate the officer's concerns. The officer will not necessarily suggest amendments but you can discuss possible alternatives to test their views. Obviously, you would need to be satisfied that any compromise would not undermine the value or purpose of your project. Where there are revisions which would satisfy the officer and would be satisfactory for you, check with them that amended drawings would be accepted by the council at whatever stage the application has reached. Significant changes might have to be subject to re-consultation and the council might be unwilling to let the application overrun while this is carried out. In those circumstances, the officer might suggest withdrawing the application (see below). Where the officer says amended drawings would be accepted, get your designer to make the alterations as quickly as possible (remembering to add a revision to the drawing reference to avoid confusion) and send them to the council.

Consultees can object to applications and what to do about this is covered in the 'Contacting consultees' section above.

You will need to weigh up any neighbour objections and decide how to respond. If they are not based on proper planning considerations, such as a supposed reduction in property value or the loss of a view, they are probably best ignored. Where there are concerns about details, like a window position, you could discuss this with the case officer and see how significant they think it is. There is then the option to revise the scheme. If neighbours raise other planning points, you can think about writing to the council to counter the objections. If you covered all the points in the objections in reasonable detail in your supporting letter/statement, there would be little to be gained by just repeating them. Only write where you can clarify or add to your case. Be objective in your response. Neighbour representations can tend towards the personal and overstated. Do not let yourself be drawn in that direction, no matter what provocation there might be. A slanging match conducted via application correspondence will not advance your proposal. Pick out the significant matters from all the representations – not responding to every small criticism will not be taken as acceptance. Give your views on each of the main points concentrating on the issue not on the person who raised it. Explain why the concerns would not actually be a problem and clarify any misunderstandings.

Where councillors request your application is decided by the planning committee, their areas of concern might be apparent in the request. You can discuss these with the case officer and write or consider amendments as appropriate. If a councillor sends an objection to the council, you can respond to it just like any other objection from a member of the public. Otherwise, you might not know about councillors' objections until the committee meeting, should your application go to committee. Unless your application is deferred or delegated at the meeting (see below), you would not get the chance to react in the current application.

Withdrawing an application

You have the right to withdraw your planning application at any point between submission and the issuing of a decision notice. This has to be done in writing. If a planning application is withdrawn, there is no fee refund but the applicant would not have to pay a fee for a resubmission, providing he or she has not already used up this exemption (see Chapter 6). There is no right of appeal where an application is withdrawn. The details of the withdrawn application remain in the council's records.

The decision on whether to withdraw has to be made in the circumstances of each case. Planning officers have an incentive to encourage applicants to withdraw applications instead of getting a refusal because it saves them having to write a report. This is not, however, likely to be a sound basis on which to make your decision. There are not many advantages for applicants to withdrawing an application. Even where you know the officer's concerns, it is still useful to have the full assessment set out in writing in an officer's report. You lose the right of appeal which limits your options, and the possibility of having an appeal to contend with could affect how an officer views a subsequent scheme. The application remains in the property's records and the fact that it was withdrawn suggests it was going to be refused so the property would not have an unblemished planning record. Where an application is going to committee, there is always a chance – even if a very small one – that it would be approved. You can also see what the councillors have to say about it which might help you frame an amended application.

Key idea

Withdrawn applications remain part of the planning history of a property.

Having made a planning application and hit a problem or opposition, but there is agreement with officers and, perhaps, neighbours on what form of development will be permitted, withdrawing can be a sensible option.

Committee meetings

As noted in Chapter 4, relatively few applications go to a council's planning committee to be decided, especially small-scale ones. Even if you do not monitor the progress of your application, the council will notify you if and when your application goes to committee. Obtain the officer's report on your application from the council's website or offices when it is made public a week or so before the meeting. Details of how to do this will be in the council's letter. Planning committee meetings are open to the public so you can attend and listen to any discussion there might be. In the absence of members of the public speaking (see below) and/or particular councillor interest, the councillors' deliberation might be brief.

The council will tell you in its letter about its rules for public speaking and might refer you to a leaflet or relevant page on its website. The circumstances in which applicants and objectors have the right to speak and the arrangements for this, including the length of time allotted and the registration requirements, will be explained. Some councils allow more than one speaker for or against applications, which enables a consultant, such as your designer or planning consultant or a supportive neighbour to speak as well as you. You can, in any event, be represented by someone else at the meeting. There is, though, no obligation for anyone to speak in support.

If your application is recommended for refusal and you have not detected any degree of councillor support, the chances are your application will be refused at the meeting. Your speaking in favour could possibly turn that around, although it is fair to say that, in most instances, the odds are against that. Do not imagine that a short speech – no matter how strongly felt or compelling the points it contains – would carry the day. Despite listening courteously, committee members sometimes give the impression that their minds are made up and are not open to persuasion. However, in the face of an application likely to go down, you have little to lose. Where objectors choose to speak against your application at the meeting, it is a good idea to speak to counter what they say. Even where your application is recommended for approval and no objectors register to speak, it can still be worth your speaking, assuming the council's rules allow it in these circumstances.

Councils generally limit public speaking to two or three minutes per person. This time span in front of a group of between a dozen to 20 people passes very quickly so be realistic in what you can convey. This is likely to translate into less than one side of text on A4 paper. Some speakers attempt to cram five minutes' worth of material into a speed-reading address which is so garbled that no listener can absorb any of it. Three to six points is all that you are likely to be able to get across, so it's better to concentrate on what you feel are the key issues. Take your cue from the officer's suggested reasons for refusal or from objections in the application file. You might find it helpful to prepare notes or write out in full what you want to say. Unless you are an accomplished presenter, speeches read out can be a little dull compared with a less scripted delivery. Councillors are lay people rather than experts and often respond better to heart-felt points and human interest aspects. Having said that, committee speeches should be on planning points and not stray into non-planning areas, like legal matters and neighbour disputes. Which issues councillors will be interested in is unpredictable and the debate might be about aspects which neither the planning officer nor objectors have mentioned.

While it is sensible to prepare a speech, be ready to depart from it if objectors say anything in their speeches that you believe needs to be countered, for example, incorrect assumptions or exaggerated claims. As with responses to written objections, do not criticize objectors but concentrate on the issues.

After any speeches by supporters and objectors there might be, the councillors will discuss your application. There is not usually any opportunity for you to respond to what they say, which can be very frustrating when it is clear they have misunderstood some vital aspect of the proposal. Finally, the councillors take a vote on the officer's recommendation and the committee's decision is made.

Focus points

* Monitor the validation of your application and check the acknowledgement letter.
* Liaise with the planning officer assigned to your case.
* Contact consultees and councillors, where appropriate.
* Encourage neighbours to write in support.
* Follow the progress of your application online.
* Take action to overcome any objections and attend the committee meeting.

Next step

Getting a favourable decision on your planning application is what you will have been working for and is, of course, the main hurdle. However, it is not necessarily the end of your dealings with the council as there are likely to be conditions with which to comply and, possibly, the need for further applications.

After planning permission is granted

In this chapter you will learn:

- ▶ *About the types of conditions attached to planning permission, and which are likely to need further approvals*
- ▶ *What 'reserved matters' are*
- ▶ *What to do if you want to make minor changes to your scheme*
- ▶ *The importance of not allowing your planning permission to expire*
- ▶ *To understand conditions*

Planning conditions

When planning permission is given, the council sends you a decision notice, which is the formal document recording the property address, the development permitted, the date of the permission and the conditions to which the permission is subject (see Figure 4.2). The conditions are important because, if you fail to comply with them, you could be in breach of the permission and at risk of enforcement action by the council and, ultimately, losing the permission.

Key idea

Planning permission is granted subject to conditions.

On receipt of the decision notice read the conditions carefully and make sure you understand them. Suggested conditions are likely to have been set out in the officer's report on your application. If any appear to be unsatisfactory, you can raise this with the planning officer during the consideration of the application. Most conditions are straightforward but they can sometimes be more complicated or written in obscure language. If there is anything in the conditions you do not understand, get in touch with the case officer to clarify what they mean and what you need to do about them.

Key idea

The approved scheme will be bound by the conditions attached to the permission.

There are several types of condition (see examples in Figure 8.1). Some require further approvals before the development permitted can be carried out (see below). Some stipulate how the development is to be carried out, such as specifying external materials to be used or the hours during which building work can be undertaken. The numbers of the approved drawings might be specified and this not only confirms what is being

No development shall be carried out unless and until samples of materials and finishes to be used for external walls and roofs of the proposed building have been submitted to and approved in writing by the Local Planning Authority. The works shall be carried out in accordance with the approved details.

No development shall take place unless and until there has been submitted to and approved in writing by the Local Planning Authority full details of both hard and soft landscaping, which shall include indications of all existing trees and hedgerows on the land, and details of those to be retained, together with measures for their protection in the course of development and these works shall be carried out as approved.

No work for the implementation of the development hereby permitted shall beundertaken on the site on Public Holidays or at any other time except between the hours of 8 am and 6 pm on Mondays to Fridays and between 8 am and 1 pm Saturdays.

The development hereby permitted shall be carried out in accordance with the approved plans listed in the schedule below.

Figure 8.1 Examples of conditions attached to a planning permission

permitted but is significant should you wish to make changes to the scheme (see below). Conditions can set out requirements that must be met before the remainder of the permission is implemented, for example the provision of visibility splays or off-street parking. Other conditions have a continuing effect. They can dictate how the development is used, such as an annexe being occupied only as part of the main house, or a garage being used only for keeping cars or domestic storage. They can limit what work is carried out subsequently, such as removing certain permitted development rights (see Chapter 2) or requiring side windows to be obscure-glazed to preserve a neighbour's privacy.

Planning permission is granted subject to a time limit for beginning the work or the use. In the case of outline permission, there is a time limit within which to submit the details of the development (see below). If the development is not begun within the time specified, it will lapse and a new application would then have to be made to get permission back again. Where your application was hard won or circumstances change, there is no guarantee that a new permission would be given or on the same terms, so it can be desirable to ensure the necessary action is taken in time in order to keep the permission alive.

Conditions requiring further approvals

There is a range of matters that can require the submission of additional information before work begins, including:

▶ samples of external building materials

▶ landscaping scheme

▶ details of access

▶ arrangements for bin storage or bicycle storage

▶ measures to protect trees during construction

▶ scheme for investigating contamination

Getting approval of such matters is generally referred to as 'discharging conditions'. It is important to obtain any approvals required by the conditions prior to actually beginning the work. If work is carried out without these conditions being discharged, the permission is not technically implemented and the development would not be lawful.

In the event that the requirements or level of detail are not clear, speak to the case officer. It might be that some requirements would have to be discussed with consultees, such as the highway authority or a council landscape officer. Where the requirements are complex or technical, you might need to employ a consultant to produce the material.

Key idea

Conditions requiring further approvals must be discharged before work starts.

You can apply to discharge conditions either in writing, giving the details of the permission, the relevant conditions and your address and contact information, or by completing a form. There is also a fee to pay and, of course, the relevant details to submit. As with planning applications, the form and guidance notes are available from the council's website or offices. More than one approval can be sought in an application. The council's fee applies to each application so applying for a number or all approvals in one application can be both administratively efficient and minimize your expenditure. The council considers the details submitted and will send you its decision.

Approval of reserved matters

Outline planning permission establishes only the principle of development, leaving some or all details to be approved subsequently. These details are the reserved matters (see Chapters 1 and 6). As noted in Chapter 6, an outline application can include some of the details and, if permission is given, those aspects will have been approved. When outline planning permission is granted, a condition specifies which of the reserved matters have yet to be approved before development begins (see Figure 8.2). A time is given within which to make that application, the standard period being three years, and a further time period by which to start work, usually two years from the date of approval of the last of the reserved matters.

Approval of the details of the means of access, appearance, layout, landscaping and scale of the buildings (hereinafter called the "reserved matters") shall be obtained from the Local Planning Authority, prior to the commencement of development on site. Application for approval of the reserved matters shall be made to the Local Planning Authority before the expiration of three years from the date of this permission. The development hereby permitted shall be begun before the expiration of two years from the date of approval of the last of the reserved matters to be approved.

Figure 8.2 Example of a reserved matters condition attached to a planning permission

Key idea
Once outline permission has been granted, the details of the scheme have to be approved.

In order to get the reserved matters approved, an application similar to a planning application has to be made to the council. In most cases it is appropriate and most efficient to apply for approval of all outstanding reserved matters in one application but you can submit the details in more than one. There is a form to complete, a fee to pay and drawings to submit. The council might have additional requirements and you should refer to the validation checklist (see Chapter 4) and speak to an officer in the planning department to ascertain what the council will need. The type and nature of drawings required is the same as for a full planning application (see Chapter 6). These show exactly what you propose to build. Those details have to be within the scope of the outline planning permission and the conditions attached to it. For example, the site area must be the same as shown in the outline application and, if there is a condition saying the building must be single storey, the proposal cannot be for a two-storey design.

While the outline permission will have got a number of issues out the way, most importantly the principle that the building can be built, there may still be many points to be resolved. These might include:

- siting of the building(s) on the site in relation to adjoining buildings and the road

- height, width and depth of building(s) to be compatible with the setting

- style of building(s) to fit in with existing or neighbouring buildings or the character of the area

- window positions to ensure privacy of neighbours

- position of the access and arrangement of parking and turning areas

- choice of external materials to be consistent with local buildings

- where planting will take place to soften the appearance of building(s) and secure privacy of neighbours

Such points can be significant matters and, in gearing up for and seeing through a reserved matters application, you might need to go through the steps set out in Chapters 5 and 7. You can submit a number of different schemes under the umbrella of an outline planning permission. It is, therefore, open to you to test alternatives, if you wish, and these could be submitted simultaneously or one after another. If a reserved matters application is refused by the council, you can reapply still under the same outline permission, provided the application is made within the timescale specified in the condition.

The council communicates its decision in a decision notice and it can add further conditions although, at this stage, they should not concern anything fundamental. When all the reserved matters have been approved, you have the equivalent of a full planning permission. Subject to getting conditions discharged and any other permissions which might be necessary, you can proceed with the project.

Non-material amendment application

After planning permission has been granted, you might wish to make minor changes to the approved scheme. Providing the changes are relatively insignificant, you can apply to vary the existing permission. The precise arrangements for getting such amendments approved are different in each of the UK countries. In England these minor changes are called 'non-material amendments'. There is no statutory definition of what constitutes a non-material amendment and it is for the council to judge what qualifies. This is dependent on the circumstances of each case, and what is considered to be non-material in one case might not be in another. Examples of councils' interpretations are given in Table 8.1. You can discuss the proposed amendments with the council to get an initial view on whether the changes qualify as non-material or whether another type of application would be appropriate.

Table 8.1 Examples of non-material and material amendments

Non-material amendments	Material amendments
Reduction in the size/volume of the building/extension	Increase in the size/volume of the building/extension
Reduction in the height of the building/extension	Increase in the height of the building/extension
Changes to windows and doors which would not have any impact on neighbouring properties	Changes which would conflict with a condition on the original approval
Minor alterations to the design of the building or minor changes to the siting of the building	New or repositioned windows and doors which would have an impact on neighbouring properties
	Changes which would alter the description of the development from the original application
	Amendments which would require re-consultation either of neighbours or other bodies

Applying for non-material amendments to an approved scheme involves submitting an application form with information about the original permission, the council's fee and amended drawings. Notice of the application must be sent to any other owners, similar to that required for a planning application (see Chapter 6). The council is not obliged to consult on or publicize these applications. The planning officers assess the proposed amendments and decide whether they would be non-material. The decision is supposed to be made within 28 days and will be sent to you. A successful non-material amendment application does not result in a new planning permission. The original permission remains in place and has to be read together with the decision letter on the non-material amendment application. There is no right of appeal against these decisions.

Minor material amendment application

Where proposed amendments to an approved scheme go beyond what is considered non-material, but those amendments would not result in a significantly different development, it is possible to apply to vary the condition which sets out the reference numbers of the approved drawings. In order to make such an application, therefore, there has to be such a condition. However, not all councils routinely include a condition setting out approved drawing numbers. If you want to make small changes, check first whether the permission does have a condition and ask the council whether this procedure would be appropriate for your circumstances. There is no statutory definition of what constitutes a minor material amendment; the government in England uses the following as a working definition:

> A minor material amendment is one whose scale and nature results in a development which is not substantially different from the one which has been approved.

This is not particularly helpful and some councils give their own criteria; examples of criteria for minor material amendments are:

▶ Would the amendment be significant in terms of its scale in relation to the original approval?

▶ Would the amendment change any use which was approved originally?

▶ Would the amendment have a detrimental impact either visually or in terms of amenity?

- Would the interests of anyone who commented on or was informed about the original application be disadvantaged in any way?

- Would the amendment be contrary to development plan policy?

- Would the amendment be contrary to another condition on the original approval?

- Would there be a significant increase in site coverage, height of building or site levels?

- Would there be additional and/or repositioned windows or doors which would have an impact on neighbouring properties?

- Would there be any change in external materials which would harm the character, appearance or quality of the development as originally approved?

- Would the amendments reverse design improvements secured during the consideration of the original application?

- Would there be greater impact on trees or any proposed landscaping scheme?

- Would there be any alteration to the application site boundary (red line)?

Remember this

Having got permission, providing there is a condition specifying drawings, you can apply to make changes before the work starts or is complete.

Minor material amendment applications are made using the same form for any type of variation or removal of a condition and the same council fee applies. The application has to be accompanied by the same sort of drawings as required for a planning application and the standard ownership certificate, with notice being served on any other owners (see Chapter 6).

In considering such applications, the council is supposed to focus on the amendments being sought, as the principle will have been established by the original permission. However, they also have to take into account any changes in planning policy or material considerations (see Chapter 3), since the original decision was taken. The council has flexibility over who to consult about the application.

If the council accepts the amendments, it issues a new decision notice giving planning permission which will repeat all the conditions (and could add new ones). The time limit within which to begin the work or use will, though, be the same as the original permission so this procedure cannot be used to extend the life of a permission. The usual rights of appeal apply to applications and decisions made under this procedure.

Maintaining planning permission

As noted earlier in this chapter, planning permissions (other than retrospective applications) are granted subject to a condition specifying a time limit within which to begin the work or use. For various reasons, you might not wish or be able to begin the work or use within that period. Where you still intend to carry out the scheme or, perhaps, to retain the benefit or value that the permission creates, you have a couple of options.

First, you can implement the permission to keep it alive. In order to do this, you need to get the conditions discharged and then carry out enough work to constitute a valid start and can then call a halt at that point. Provided the permission has been implemented properly, it will remain available for you to complete when you choose. If using this route, it is desirable to record the work carried out and when it was done, including taking dated photos, and to get documentary evidence, such as a contractor's invoice, and keep this in a safe place. It is ideal to get confirmation from the council that the permission has been implemented if you can. One way of doing this is to arrange for an inspection to be made by a building control officer in connection with building regulations approval. A note of the inspection should be retained in the council's records. Sometimes planning officers can be persuaded to confirm that work has begun.

Remember this

Take action to keep your permission alive before it lapses.

The law says what development has to be carried out in order to initiate a planning permission:

- construction work in the course of the erection of a building

- work of demolition of a building

- digging a trench which is to contain the foundations, or part of the foundations, of a building

- laying of any underground main or pipe to the foundations, or part of the foundations, of a building or to a foundation trench

- operations in the course of laying out or constructing a road or part of a road

- any change in the use of any land (other than a change of use allowed as permitted development)

Second, you can reapply to keep permission alive, which is often described as applying for 'renewal' of planning permission. This can be slightly misleading because the considerations which apply in deciding a 'renewal' application are the same as for any other application. While the existence of a planning permission still in place is helpful and a significant point, it does not guarantee another permission would be given. Providing circumstances have not changed since the earlier permission was granted, there would be no reason for refusal. However, any differences in circumstances, for example, changes in planning policy or government guidance, recent planning appeal decisions, new developments carried out, trees or screening removed or changes in the area, could potentially affect the decision. If the council's requirements for financial contributions have changed or a Community Infrastructure Levy has come into effect, you would be caught by the new provisions.

If you think it is likely you will need to apply for a new permission, it is a good idea to reapply in plenty of time just in case the council considers circumstances have changed and refuses permission. This would give the opportunity to discharge any conditions and begin work, as described above, before the existing permission expires. The application requirements for 'renewal' applications are different in each of the UK countries. Check what is needed with your council as you would for any other application (see Chapter 6).

Paying financial contributions

Where planning permission is granted with a legal agreement to pay financial contributions (see Chapters 4 and 6), the document you signed will set out at what point the money has to be paid. This might be when the work begins to implement the permission, before the building is occupied or at some other point in the process or within a specified time period of one of these events. The payment might be made in instalments with certain percentages due at different times. Make sure you note when the payment is due as it is your responsibility to pay it. Check with the council what arrangements or options there are for paying the sum. When paying, include the planning application reference number and property address. State clearly that it is a payment required by a legal agreement and give the date of the document.

If your council has a Community Infrastructure Levy (CIL) in place and your proposal is caught by it, you will have completed a form when the application was submitted (see Chapter 6). When granting planning permission, the council sends a Liability Notice which sets out the amount to be paid when the development commences, the payment procedure and the possible consequences, if this procedure is not followed. Responsibility for paying CIL, like planning permission, lies with the ownership of land. Charges made under CIL are due for payment from the date when the development begins in accordance with the planning permission. If a council wants to establish its own payment deadlines and/or give the option to pay by instalments, it can do so by publishing an instalments policy on its website. The person carrying out the development serves a Commencement Notice on the council when construction begins. The council then serves a Demand Notice for the CIL. If development starts without a Commencement Notice, penalties apply and CIL is payable immediately.

Focus points

✻ Check the planning conditions, in particular the time limits.

✻ Apply to the council to discharge any conditions that require further approvals.

✻ Get the details (reserved matters) approved by the council after obtaining outline planning permission. Submit an application if you need to amend the approved scheme.

✻ Keep your planning permission alive.

✻ Pay any financial contributions due on time.

Next step

These are the steps you need to take once your planning application has been approved. However, not every application is given permission or is free from adverse restrictions. There are ways to overcome unsatisfactory decisions.

Dealing with unsatisfactory decisions

In this chapter you will learn:

- ▶ *What to do if you object to planning conditions*
- ▶ *What to do if planning permission is refused*
- ▶ *When and how to revise and resubmit an application*
- ▶ *How to decide whether or not to appeal*

Adverse conditions

Even though planning permission might have been given, the conditions to which that permission is subject might make it unacceptable to you. Examples could include a limit on the number of storeys on an outline application, a requirement to close an access point, removal of permitted development rights, being obliged to make certain windows obscure-glazed or an additional survey and report having to be submitted to the council. Sometimes a condition will require something to be done on someone else's land before the development begins, such as provision of a visibility splay at an access point. In these circumstances, you would need the consent of the other landowner as the grant of planning permission does not give you any rights over someone else's property. If the neighbour is not prepared to co-operate, the permission cannot be implemented validly.

Remember this

When planning permission is granted, check conditions carefully to ensure they are acceptable.

Initially, discuss any unacceptable planning conditions with the case officer. With delegated decisions, you might not get advance notice of what conditions are going to be imposed, although you might have an indication through your communications with the officer during the consideration of the application. Also, consultees can suggest conditions and, by monitoring the application, you can pick these up and contact the case officer or consultee if any suggested condition would cause you problems. With committee decisions, the case officer's report, published before the meeting, sets out what conditions he or she recommends and so you have an opportunity to attempt to head them off by making representations to the officer and the committee. The council is obliged to give a reason for imposing each condition but these might be quite vague. Ask the officer why the condition(s) in question was considered necessary, whether any alternative might meet your needs and the council's concern and, if relevant, clarify exactly what it would take to satisfy the condition.

Faced with an unacceptable condition, you have several options. First, you can review your proposal and decide whether you would be able to live with the condition after all, or to accept it in the short term and try to overturn it at some point in the future. Second, you can make an application to vary or remove the condition. There is a specific form to complete for these applications. In the application you would explain why the condition as imposed is inappropriate or defective and what difficulties it would cause. Conditions are supposed to pass certain tests (see Chapter 4) and you can make a case based on the failure of the offending condition to do so. Where a consultee has asked for the condition, see if you can agree a variation with that body and get it to confirm any agreement in writing so you can submit it in support of your application. In some cases, the council will be sympathetic and prepared to vary or remove a condition altogether. Having considered it reasonable, though, the council might well be resistant to changing it. Third, you have a right of appeal against a condition(s) attached to a planning permission (see Chapter 4). If the planning officer is adamant that the council would not vary or remove an unacceptable condition, an appeal against the condition is likely to be the best option available to you. Also, if an application to vary or remove a condition is refused permission by the council, you can appeal against that decision. Appeals on these bases are very similar and the arguments are going to be the same in either case. In the case of an appeal against a refused application to change a condition, you are likely to have a more detailed explanation of the council's thinking on the need for the condition during the application process and so have more to get your teeth into when lodging the appeal. With this type of appeal, the original permission cannot be overturned whereas, in theory, with an appeal against the imposition of a condition, the inspector can overturn the original permission.

Should the scheme go ahead without compliance with one or more conditions, depending on the particular condition(s), either the permission will not have been initiated validly or it will be in breach of the condition(s). If this came to the attention of the council, it might take action. One of the possible actions it could take is to serve a breach of condition notice. There is no right of planning appeal against a breach of condition notice; it can only be challenged in a magistrate's court.

Reasons for refusal

When planning permission is refused, the decision notice sets out the council's reasons for refusal. In some instances, the stated reason will not be the real reason permission was refused. For example, if neighbours and councillors are concerned about increased on-street parking and congestion in the road but the highway authority has not objected on those grounds, the council might be apprehensive about giving a reason for refusal unsupported by the technical expert opinion of the highway officers. Were the applicant to appeal, the council might be vulnerable to a cost claim for refusing permission unreasonably. In these circumstances, the council might find some other more subjective pretext on which to refuse permission, such as design.

Remember this

Study and research reasons for refusal to ascertain whether and how they can be overcome.

Read each reason carefully. They will be written in planning jargon and will quote planning policies, the combination of which could mean it is difficult for you to discern precisely what is meant. Get hold of the planning officer's report, if you have not seen it already. By studying this, you should get the gist of the officer's objections and so make sense of the reasons for refusal. If you do not understand the reasons given, speak to the planning officer and ask him or her to explain them to you in layman's terms.

Consider the reasons and whether the council's position appears reasonable. Look up the policies and guidance quoted in the reasons and see whether the council has a point. Some policies are specific, such as those stating locations where new development will not be allowed or giving minimum dwelling space standards. Others are subjective, such as ones requiring a high standard of design or preserving neighbours' amenities. In the latter case, the degree of compliance with the policy is dependent on matters of opinion.

Reasons for refusal fall into two categories – principle and detail (see Figures 9.1 and 9.2) – and the distinction is important for how to tackle them. Principle-based reasons will be that it is the wrong sort of proposal and/or in the wrong place and will be fundamental to the scheme. Detail-based reasons could be, for example, that the design or materials are wrong, a window overlooks a neighbour, the building is too tall or a necessary legal agreement has not been signed. There could be a mix of the two types of reasons for refusal.

The proposal would constitute inappropriate development, detrimental to the open character of the Green Belt and would thereby conflict with Policies SP6 and RO2 of the Haydon Local Plan.

The proposed dwelling would, by virtue of the overdevelopment of this very constrained site, proximity to neighbouring amenity space, limited plot size and lack of parking, result in a cramped, poorly spaced and poorly landscaped development which would have a detrimental impact on the character of the area and lead to a loss of privacy and increased noise and disturbance to the detriment of residential amenities of neighbouring occupiers, contrary to Policies ST2, ST5 & ST14 of the Belldown District Local Plan.

Figure 9.1 Examples of reasons for refusal on principle

In the opinion of the Local Planning Authority the proposed dwelling by reason of its excessive size and height in comparison to nearby buildings would fail to respond to local character or be visually attractive in its context. The proposal therefore fails to accord with the requirements of Policy 75 of the Easthampton District Local Plan or central government planning policy requiring good design as set out in Section 7 of the National Planning Policy Framework.

The proposed extension by reason of its siting and design would have a harmful effect on the living conditions currently enjoyed by the residents and occupiers of adjoining dwellings because it would result in loss of privacy and loss of outlook and light. As such the proposed development is contrary to Local Plan Policies B2, B5, H16, H17.

Figure 9.2 Examples of reasons for refusal on detail

Reasons for refusal are supposed to be the precise concerns the council has. One well-targeted reason can be a sufficient basis on which to turn down permission. Some councils, however, adopt a belt-and-braces approach and go for volume with reasons for refusal. Therefore, do not be put off by the number of reasons given but concentrate on the content and separate objections they contain.

Resubmission of an application

Having considered the reasons for refusal, if you think those reasons can be overcome, it is usually appropriate to revise and resubmit your application. This is more likely to be the case where a refusal of planning permission is based on the details of the scheme. The first application should give you good pointers for making amendments. The officer's report, neighbours' letters and consultees' responses could all contain useful information to help you refine your proposal in a way that would enable the council to support it second time around. Sometimes, in difficult circumstances, it might take a number of attempts to come up with a scheme that gets permission. It sometimes happens that the case officer changes from one application to the next. If you are unlucky, a new case officer might have different views from the previous one and so you cannot be guaranteed a consistent approach.

Key idea

Resubmission is often a faster route to getting permission than an appeal.

On the face of it, refusals based on principle are less likely to be approved on resubmission to the council. There could, however, be instances where circumstances change, for example, a different policy comes into effect, other permissions are granted or a helpful appeal decision is issued. Alternatively, there could be arguments which were not made in a first application that could be advanced in a subsequent one. Be realistic in your assessment of principle-based reasons for refusal and only use the resubmission route where you feel, or the officers suggest, there is a fair chance it will be approved.

A revised application after refusal is a new planning application and you should follow the steps set out in Chapters 5–7. In particular, if you can, discuss the revisions with the case officer in advance of resubmission. In a resubmission application, your letter/ statement should include a section or paragraph on each reason for refusal and explain how the revised proposal overcomes the concern raised. You could consider highlighting on the application drawings how the amended scheme differs from the previous one. This could, perhaps, include showing the outline of the previously proposed building dotted on the drawing of the new building to illustrate changes such as in siting, ridge height or roof shape.

There is a council application fee exemption for resubmissions, often referred to as a 'free go'. The qualifications for this are:

▶ It is made within 12 months of the decision (application or appeal) on the previous application.

▶ It is made within 12 months of submission of the previous application which was withdrawn.

- It is the first revision.
- The application site is the same.
- The person applying is the same.
- The character or description of the proposal is the same.

When to appeal

There are various circumstances in which there is a right of appeal. You can appeal against:

- refusal of planning permission;
- conditions attached to planning permission;
- non-determination, where the council does not decide an application within the target timescale;
- refusal to approve reserved matters;
- refusal of approval required by a condition;
- failure to validate an application.

If the council refuses your planning application and some or all of the reasons for refusal relate to the principle of the proposal, or you are not prepared to accept the compromises which would be necessary to overcome reasons which relate to detail, consider making an appeal. Except, possibly, for householder appeals (see Chapter 4), resubmission of a planning application is likely to result in a quicker decision than an appeal. It is usually best to explore with the council whether there is scope to negotiate a permission with them rather than to appeal. However, there are many instances where it is evident the council is very unlikely to change its mind.

Remember this

When the council is unlikely to give planning permission, you can use your right of appeal to try to overturn a refusal.

Before deciding whether to appeal, weigh up each of the reasons for refusal carefully and be certain you would have a plausible case to put forward to counter them. In particular, look up all policies referred to in the reasons. Councils tend to put relatively more weight on their own policies than on government guidance, whereas planning inspectors tend to give full weight to government guidance. The council might not mention government guidance in its reasons for refusal so it is worth looking into that guidance. See whether there is anything which would help your case and, potentially, contradict the council's policy, especially where the government guidance is more recent than the council's policy.

Deciding whether to appeal against non-determination of your application can be harder to judge. If you wait and let the council make a decision, you have two chances of success (the application and an appeal). If you are monitoring the application, you might have a fair idea of whether the officer is going to support the proposal. If you detect support, it might be appropriate to hold off on an appeal. When you have no faith that the council will make a decision within a reasonable period, an appeal is a way to bring matters to a head. Bear in mind that the appeal process is likely to take a while to produce a decision, so weigh this against the likely timescale for a council decision. You can phone the Planning Inspectorate (or equivalent bodies in Scotland and Northern Ireland) to get an idea of how long appeals are taking.

The governments of the UK and/or the respective appeal bodies publish guidance on the appeal process, available on their websites, from their offices or, some of it, from council offices. Read this before undertaking an appeal to make sure you understand what is involved and can comply with the various requirements. There are timetables to follow and stages when action is needed. This can also help you decide whether to use a consultant (see below).

Except in Northern Ireland, there is currently no fee charged for making an appeal. The two sides in an appeal are normally expected to pay their own costs of going to appeal, for example, planning consultants' fees. However, there is provision for councils and appellants to ask for an award of costs against the other side (see Chapter 4). If such an application is made, the inspector who decides the appeal also makes a decision on whether an award of cost is justified in the circumstances of the case. Costs are awarded where three factors are all present:

▶ One party (council or appellant) makes a claim at the right time.

▶ A party has acted unreasonably.

▶ The unreasonable behaviour has cost the other party money or wasted time.

Key idea

Councils and appellants can claim costs of going to appeal but only where the other party has been unreasonable.

In England, inspectors can also initiate an award of costs, even where neither party makes a claim. Costs awards are rare but something to bear in mind before deciding whether to appeal. The crucial point is what constitutes 'unreasonable' in this context and examples are given in Table 4.1.

Professional help

When planning permission is refused, or approved with an unacceptable condition attached, could be the time to get a planning consultant involved. If the refusal can be overcome by just tweaking the scheme and resubmitting an application, that could be straightforward and you can probably deal with it, working with your designer. Where the objections are more substantial or you do not feel inclined to compromise, you might need help in weighing up the options. You could, if you wish, commission a planning consultant to give an opinion on the circumstances and the courses of action open to you and the advantages of each.

Where a reason for refusal relates to a specialist area, for example, impact on trees, ecology or highways, you might need to find a consultant to advise you on that aspect (see Chapter 5). It could be that you would need to commission an opinion or report which would tell you whether the objection is well founded or can be overcome and provide the evidence necessary to accompany a resubmitted application or an appeal.

Key idea

At the point when planning permission is refused is often the time to employ a planning consultant.

While applications can be complicated, there are still aspects a layman could take on and deal with successfully. However, appeals are more technical. There are procedures to follow and issues need to be dealt with precisely and on proper planning grounds. With written appeals, the only opportunity to influence the inspector is through the documents submitted so your personal qualities will not come into it. Small-scale residential applications, such as extensions or single houses, are likely to be dealt with using the householder appeal service, or in writing, rather than by a hearing or inquiry. The latter two methods involve more procedure and, although you are not obliged to be professionally represented, in most cases it would be somewhat reckless for people with no previous experience to attempt to deal with them on their own. The procedure for householder appeals is simplest but you still need to prepare grounds of appeal. Appeal decisions are an important part of the planning history of a site and a badly handled appeal could result in a decision which makes it that much harder to get permission for what you want. As a result, it is generally best to get the advice of a planning consultant on an appeal, even if you choose to do some of the work yourself.

Focus points

* Study conditions to check they are acceptable.
* Carefully analyse reasons for refusal. Consider revising and resubmit an application to overcome objections.
* Decide whether to appeal against a refusal.
* Get professional help to deal with refusal of permission.

Next step

This section has dealt with how to maximize your chances of making a successful planning application. There are circumstances in which you might need to protect your home or area from someone else's development. This is covered in the next section and the first step is to be aware of what is happening in your neighbourhood.

PART 3
PROTECTING YOUR PROPERTY

Knowing what is happening

In this chapter you will learn:

▶ *How to find out about new development proposals in your area*
▶ *The benefits of keeping in touch with special interest groups and the parish council*

New development, whether it is something quite small, like alterations to a neighbour's house, or something major, such as a new housing estate, road or industrial area nearby, can adversely affect your quality of life and the value of your property. All too often, though, protests about new development start when the bulldozers or builders move in, which is far too late. The optimum times to influence new development are when local plan policies are revised and when a planning application is made. This section takes you through all the steps you can take to identify and make effective representations regarding a planning application that might affect your interests. It also describes the actions you should take where development goes ahead without planning permission.

Where to find information on local development proposals

LOCAL PLAN POLICIES

The locations of large-scale developments, such as new housing estates, industrial areas, retail parks and new roads are generally determined in the local plan. A key aspect of protecting your property is to keep an eye out for reviews of local plan policies in your area. When a site is allocated for say, housing, in the local plan, you will have an uphill task later, at the planning application stage, to resist that new housing altogether. You might be able to influence the layout and precise design of the development but the principle of housing would have been firmly established. Similar sentiments apply to development allocated through a neighbourhood plan. Public consultation is an important part of local and neighbourhood plan preparation as is the opportunity to formally object to a local plan. Neighbourhood plans are the subject of a public referendum, so there is scope to directly influence their adoption through voting. Chapter 3 sets out the opportunities for making your views known when these policy documents are the subject of public consultation.

In addition to allocating specific areas for housing and employment-generating uses, local plans establish the boundaries of specially designated areas such as Conservation Areas, Areas of

Outstanding Natural Beauty, Green Belt and so on. In addition to these national designations, there are also likely to be local designations, including development boundaries, primary and secondary shopping areas, and local landscape and townscape protection areas to which particular policies apply. It is a good idea to keep an eye on all these designations when local plans are reviewed, to see if special designations are being introduced, extended or removed in your area. If you live in an area close to, but not in, a Conservation Area or other landscape or townscape protection area, then lobbying to have that area extended to include your property would provide additional protection for the character and appearance of the area and, therefore, the setting of your house.

You can find out about local and neighbourhood plan preparation and the opportunities to make your views known by looking at the council's website or speaking to its planning policy department. These plans are subject to wide public consultation so there are also likely to be local exhibitions, reviews in local papers and, possibly, mail shots to local residents.

Remember this

You can influence the policies on which planning decisions are based.

PLANNING APPLICATIONS

Planning applications have to be publicized with a view to obtaining the views of neighbours and the local community. This includes all forms of planning application, whether detailed or outline, householder or major scheme, Conservation Area or listed building consent and advertisement, and waste disposal. There are various ways in which applications are publicized. Knowing where and when publicity takes place, and how to check on applications generally in your area, ensures you are aware of what is going on and so are able to have your say.

PRE-APPLICATION COMMUNITY CONSULTATION

In England and Wales, developers of large-scale housing and other projects are obliged to undertake a pre-application consultation exercise and to submit a Statement of Community Involvement with their applications. This might involve local exhibitions and meetings, or simply comprise questionnaires sent to local residents. Scotland has its own system of consultation which includes compulsory public meetings for large-scale developments, which must be publicized in a local paper.

Developers are expected to show how their proposals have been amended to reflect local opinion, so make sure you, and others potentially affected by a development, participate in the exercise and make your views known.

NOTIFICATION LETTERS

In England and Wales, councils write to immediate neighbours to inform them of planning applications nearby. Precisely who is an immediate neighbour is not defined and these letters cannot be relied upon to notify you of development proposals close enough to your property to affect your amenities. In Northern Ireland, neighbours within 90 metres are automatically notified. In Scotland, addresses within 20 metres of the site are notified and, if there are none, a notice advertising the application is published in a local paper. Notification letters give the address and a very brief description of the proposed development, the reference number of the application and the date by which any representations should be made.

SITE NOTICES AND LOCAL NEWSPAPER ADVERTS

All planning applications, from the most humble domestic extension through to national infrastructure, have to be publicized to make members of the public aware of them and to give them the opportunity to comment. One of the most conspicuous methods of publicity is site notices. These are posted outside properties where applications are in progress. They are generally white or brightly-coloured A4 posters which state the address of the property concerned, the proposed development and the date by which any comments or objections should be made. While they are an eye-catching way to publicize applications, they are not used everywhere, nor are they compulsory. So, apart from the obvious risk of any notice being vandalized or succumbing to the weather, they are not an infallible guide to what is going on.

> ### Remember this
>
> Do not rely on the council notifying you of planning applications or posting a notice on the site.

COUNCIL'S WEEKLY LIST

A reliable source of information is the council's weekly list of applications, which is published in a local newspaper (usually under 'public notices'), posted on the planning section of the council's website, available at the planning department and often sent to parish councils and libraries. One point to watch with these lists is that, where you live near district boundaries, it might be necessary to monitor more than one council list in order to be sure you are picking up all the applications in your neighbourhood. Another challenge that comes with larger-scale schemes is that the address given for them may not clearly identify where they are. 'Land west of High Street' or 'land fronting Maple Avenue' for example, could be the seemingly innocuous titles for large sites which extend many hundreds of metres from the roads that are mentioned. With any current application it should be a simple matter to look up the application site location plan which will show, edged in red, the extent of the site. A final challenge is that the brief description of the proposed development could hide a multitude of sins. An outline application for 'housing' could refer to 4 or 500 houses. Again, unless a description is clear and specific, take a moment to look up the application documents so you know exactly what is proposed.

In addition to the weekly list, applications are published on councils' websites and can be accessed via the planning application search facility. The online records usually include the application forms, accompanying plans and any reports or statements. Online search facilities vary in user-friendliness. Some ask for the application reference but others are searchable using a wide range of terms, including house and road names, and postcodes. The latter are helpful in alerting you to any applications in your immediate vicinity.

Remember this
The details of planning applications should be available on council websites.

PARISH COUNCILS AND LOCAL INTEREST GROUPS
Parish councils are consulted on applications and consider their merits at parish meetings. All applications in the parish are considered by the parish council and, increasingly, parish councils have websites on which details of applications may be published and news posted of anything potentially contentious. Similarly, local interest groups, such as conservation societies, environmental protection groups and residents' associations, monitor and make representations on applications which affect their particular interests. To the extent these groups address matters of concern to you, keep in touch with them and even consider joining them, as this helps you to keep abreast of development proposals in your area and to identify those that might be contentious or harmful to your interests.

NATIONAL SPECIAL INTEREST GROUPS
There are national groups which monitor applications and routinely object to any that affect their interests. Examples include the Ramblers Association and Open Spaces Society which are concerned with the maintenance of open spaces, public access and public footpaths. Others, like Campaign for the Protection of Rural England and Friends of the Earth, have a more general environmental and ecological protection remit. The Georgian Group is concerned with the conservation of historic buildings and landscapes. Such organizations might monitor applications for those that significantly affect their interests but do not rely on them to pick up on every relevant application. Consider joining any group which campaigns on issues important to you in order to find out about developments that might concern you, or see what information regarding local development schemes is published on their websites.

CHECKING THE COUNCIL'S WEBSITE

As well as posting the weekly lists of applications, council websites often publicize details of applications of particular public interest in either the general or planning news section of the site. A few councils have an alert system, whereby you can set up automatic emailed alerts when certain types of applications in specified locations are made.

LOCAL NEWSPAPER STORIES

Large-scale and potentially contentious development proposals are generally publicized in local newspapers. One advantage of these stories is that they sometimes give advance notice of proposals before they get to the formal planning application stage as a result of developers' pre-application consultation (see above). These sorts of consultations might be publicized in local papers but not widely elsewhere. The disadvantage of local papers is that information is not always accurate and should be verified either by checking with the district council or by contacting the developer direct.

INTERNET SEARCHES

While internet searches are a great source of information generally, they do not work so well when you do not know what it is you are searching for. Seeking information about a particular site or development proposal could well prove productive, but casting about trying to find out if there is anything of significance which might affect your property is likely to be inefficient and certainly not reliable.

COUNCIL'S ENFORCEMENT OFFICER

Where development is taking place apparently without planning permission, the council's enforcement officer is the person who should know what is going on, whether a planning application is likely to be forthcoming or whether enforcement action is on the cards. It is not uncommon for planning applications to be made retrospectively where development has gone ahead, knowingly or not, without the necessary permission in place. Enforcement officers usually set a time limit for an application to be made and should be prepared to tell you what the likely timing for an application might be. This enables you to get a head start on preparing your objection and also ensures you are ready for the application when it is submitted.

Alternatively, the development might be considered sufficiently harmful that either an enforcement notice should be served to prevent it from continuing or, in extreme cases, a stop notice served to bring the use or building works to an instant halt. In both these cases be alert for an appeal, which would have to be lodged within 28 days of an enforcement notice being served.

Remember this

Contact the council's planning enforcement officer for information about development without planning permission.

Focus points

* Be aware of development proposals in your area.
* Check local and neighbourhood plan policies for your area.
* Look out for site notices and newspaper adverts, and read the council's weekly list of planning applications.
* Keep in touch with special interest groups and the parish council.
* Contact the council's enforcement officer if development is taking place without planning permission.

Next step

Once you are aware that development is planned or taking place in your neighbourhood, you need to know in what ways you can object to or influence how or whether it takes place.

Making objections

In this chapter you will learn:

▶ *When it is appropriate to object to an application*
▶ *What the time limits are for making your objection*
▶ *How to make an objection*

Circumstances for objections

When a planning application is made for something that you are not happy with, you have the right to object. It is commonplace for objections to be made by neighbours and local residents to development proposals which might directly affect their interests. There is, though, nothing stopping anyone from objecting to any application, regardless of where it is. In addition to making a formal objection as part of the planning application process, you can approach other consultees direct, such as the parish council or highway authority, and lobby local councillors or your MP. Exceptionally, you might be able to get an application taken out of the hands of the local council and decided by the government, under the so-called 'call-in' procedure.

Key idea

It is common for neighbours and local residents to object to planning applications.

There are different types of planning application that might be of interest to you. These are:

► full or detailed applications;

► outline applications;

► applications for approval of reserved matters;

► applications to remove or amend conditions;

► applications to renew temporary planning permissions;

► applications for waste processing or disposal;

► applications for minerals extraction;

► applications for demolition.

In addition to these applications, be alert for applications related to permitted development, where applicants must notify the council before they go ahead with the build or change of use. The most significant of these so-called 'prior notification' situations (in England) is where your neighbours want to build a large rear extension to their property. The council must notify the adjoining neighbours and ask whether there are any objections, giving you the opportunity to make your views known. The prior notification procedure also applies to certain types of agricultural permitted development and to a range of changes of use, although with the latter the council can only consider the proposal against a very limited range of criteria, such as whether the property is in a flood risk area.

Before you think about objecting, consider contacting the person or organization making the application to see if there is scope to modify the scheme to address your concerns. This is unlikely to be effective if you are concerned about the principle of the development but, if it is a relatively minor detail, like the position of a window or some aspect of the parking layout, then you might be able to resolve the issue. Applicants might not be happy to hear from a potential objector and could be defensive but, equally, they might be keen to co-operate to avoid controversy and potentially bad publicity. If you do decide to contact the applicant, do so in as friendly and constructive a way as you can, so as to increase your chances of developing a fruitful dialogue.

Applications for developments that are ill-advised, poorly designed or likely to be harmful are normally rejected by the council, regardless of whether anybody objects. Occasionally such schemes do slip through the net and get approved, so it is still worthwhile objecting, even if you are pointing out what appear to be obvious and fatal defects.

Remember this

Do not assume schemes with obvious defects will be refused permission.

Where an application threatens a non-listed historic building, you can apply to get it listed, so increasing the chances of it being preserved. In England, apply to English Heritage; in Scotland, Historic Scotland; in Wales, CADW (Welsh Historic Monuments Executive Agency); and in Northern Ireland, the Northern Ireland Environment Agency. Buildings can be listed instantly (known as spot-listing) giving the relevant agency time to consider the building's merits and suitability for listing. Listing would almost certainly prevent demolition and would bring much tighter regulation over extensions and alterations, and also over any proposed development near to the building that might affect its setting.

Facilities of particular benefit to a community, such as pubs, libraries or sports grounds, can be designated as Assets of Community Value (in England only at the time of writing). You can request the council designates a particular asset, either in response to a planning application or because you think the facility is vulnerable to re-development – perhaps because it is vacant or becoming run-down. Once designated, the property has greater protection.

Applications to fell trees subject to tree preservation orders (TPO) are dealt with in a similar manner to planning applications, although are less well advertised. You can object to an application to fell a protected tree or, where an attractive or significant tree is to be felled as part of a planning application, you can lobby the council to get a TPO imposed on it. This does not prevent a tree from being felled, as a planning permission overrides a TPO, but it does ensure that much closer scrutiny is given to the merits of retaining the tree and, if it is to be lost, to replacing it or otherwise compensating for its loss.

When a planning application is refused, the applicant has a right to appeal. All objections made at the application stage are passed on to the appeal inspector and will be taken into account. You can make further objections as part of the appeal process, except in the case of householder appeals in England and Wales, where no further comments are allowed.

Where planning permission is granted, it is generally subject to conditions. You can monitor the progress of a development and alert the council if you think the works are departing from the approved scheme or you suspect there are breaches of conditions.

In addition, where you suspect development is taking place without planning permission and it is adversely affecting you or your community's interests, you can contact the council's enforcement section to register your concerns. Councils do not actively police development and are reliant on the public to make complaints or notify them of development that appears to be unlawful. Some building works or changes of use might not require permission, or be permitted development, and so are entirely lawful. The council can clarify this, if there is doubt. In addition, since planning permissions remain alive indefinitely once the works have commenced, it is possible for a development to suddenly re-activate where permission was granted and implemented (i.e. started) many years, even decades, ago. If the development is not lawful, the council might initiate enforcement proceedings. Where an enforcement notice is served, requiring a use or building to be modified or to cease, the developer has a right of appeal. As with refused planning applications, members of the public can make their opinions known as part of that appeal process.

Key idea

Councils rely on members of the public to inform them of unlawful development.

As well as taking positive action against unlawful development, it is possible to influence the scope of permitted development, for things like extensions and alteration to buildings and many changes of use, in certain circumstances. The mechanism for this is an 'Article 4 Direction' (see Chapter 2). If you are concerned about a particular type of permitted development that either is or could cause harm in your area, you can ask the council to consider imposing an Article 4 Direction. There is no formal mechanism for making such a request and it would be a matter of speaking to officers and writing to the council. You can seek a direction on a single building or piece of land, or on a whole neighbourhood, as appropriate. Examples of where an Article 4 Direction might be appropriate include in Conservation Areas to restrict changes to buildings and so preserve the character and appearance of the area, or in the countryside to remove rights to put up fencing, so preventing the fragmentation of land sold off as 'leisure plots'. An Article 4 Direction would not necessarily prevent changes from taking place, ultimately, but it would mean that planning permission would be needed for those changes, giving you the opportunity to formally object if and when an application was made.

Where and how to see applications

Once you are aware a planning application has been made, you can look at the submitted forms, plans and any accompanying statements. These can be found on the council's website via their planning application search facility or viewed at the council's offices. Parish councils also sometimes make copies of applications available to view and drawings might be held at local libraries. Where an application includes very large drawings, it can be advantageous to view full-scale paper copies as large drawings can be difficult to decipher on a small computer screen. If the drawings are difficult to understand, most councils have a duty planning officer available who can take you through them and answer any queries. You can buy copies of planning applications from the council, if you wish to take drawings away to study in detail, or you can download from the council's website and print them yourself.

In addition to looking at the planning application itself, you can usually also see comments from consultees, such as neighbours, the parish council or the highway authority, which might help you to shape your own objections. Do not wait too long to find out what every other consultee is saying before lodging your objection though, as you might fall foul of time limits.

Time limits for objecting

Once you have had a look at the application, it is important to find out the time period for making objections. This is given on notification letters sent to neighbours, on site notices and on the council's online record of the application, which will normally say that objections should be made within 21 days of the application being registered or 21 days of when a notice is posted. Most council websites have an online objection facility and this might close once the 21 days is up. Although it is advisable to make your objection within the stated time period, any objection made up to the date of the decision should be taken into account. If you are unable to make your objection within the time period, contact the application case officer to check that a late objection will still be considered. If, for whatever reason, the officer were to say your written objection would be too late, this should not prevent you from discussing your concerns with him or her to ensure they are understood.

With planning appeals there is a rigid time frame for objections to be made, set out in notification letters. In England, this is within five weeks of the start date of the appeal. Objections sent in after the specified date are liable to be returned unread.

Remember this

Be aware of the time limits set by the council and at appeal for objections to be lodged, and stick to them.

How to make your objection

In order to get your objection formally included as part of the application papers, it must be made in writing. You can post or email an objection or make it online on the council's website. However you object, make sure the application reference and site address are clearly displayed, so that your objection is registered against the right application. Bear in mind that your objection will be placed on the application file and, therefore, be in the public realm where the applicant in particular is likely to read it. Be clear about whether your objection is to the very principle of what is proposed or to just a part of it, or whether you are merely seeking an amendment to the scheme or the imposition of conditions to prevent any harmful impact on your property or amenities. Most councils produce guidance on how to object, with lists of relevant issues to focus on and factors that will not be taken into account. They also caution against defamatory or libellous statements, so beware of attacking the developer's motives or track record. Stick to the concerns you have with the development in question (see Chapter 12).

CONTACTING PLANNING OFFICERS

You can speak to the case officer before making your objection. If there is anything you do not understand or you wish to discuss your concerns first, phone the officer or make an appointment to meet him or her. Where a proposed development would have a direct effect on your home, invite the officer to come and view the situation from your property, so he or she can fully appreciate the likely impact. While, in many cases, the site visit and the officer's consideration of the proposal happen towards the end of the application period, make sure you get your request in at the beginning, in case the officer is making an early site inspection. After submitting your objection, to give it extra force, you can phone to check the case officer has read and understood your points. Phoning an officer too soon risks catching them before they have got to grips with the application, too late and they have already formed an opinion. Responses from officers vary, from the relaxed and chatty to the tight-lipped and unresponsive. Where the officer is unwilling to discuss your objection, berating them is unlikely to increase their sympathies for your concerns, as is threatening to 'go over their head' to a manager or head of department. There might, though, be occasions when going over their head is advisable, for example, where you encounter an inexperienced officer who seems unable or unwilling to grasp your concerns. Do adopt a friendly attitude towards planning officers and endeavour to build rapport. However upset you might be by an application, remember it is the officer's job to look at all sides of the argument for and against, so do not expect them automatically to be swayed by your particular concerns, no matter how strongly felt.

Remember this

Lodge your objection in writing but follow it up with a phone call to the planning officer.

CONTACTING OTHER CONSULTEES

Parish councils are consultees on planning applications but do not decide the outcome. Nonetheless, some parish councils give the impression they are decision takers, by having a dedicated planning committee which considers applications and makes a decision to object or support the proposals. Some consider planning applications as part of their regular meetings while others do so less formally, with a small group of councillors meeting to run through the schemes. You should be able to attend and speak at the more formal meetings. It is well worth doing this, as objections to a development from neighbours can be undermined if the parish comes out in favour. Bear in mind that parish councillors, on the whole, know very little about planning policy and even less about planning law. Therefore, focus the objections you make to the parish council on practical issues that can be understood from a common sense point of view. Getting parish councillors out to look at the situation from your property is a good idea, enabling them to see the likely problems and for you to build rapport with them. All of this needs to be done very early in the application process, as parish councils, like all other consultees, are asked to get their views to the planning officer within three weeks of the start of the application.

The opinion of the parish council might influence the local district councillor, who could also be a parish councillor. Do not neglect the parish council as it is an important link in the political chain. If neighbour objections are supported by the parish, and the parish's views are supported by the district councillor, then the councillor can either influence the planning officer or directly promote the objectors' viewpoint at planning committee.

Where your objection relates to something on which the council is seeking advice from a specialist consultee, such as the highway authority or Environment Agency, there is nothing to stop you contacting that consultee direct and discussing your concerns. If you write or email, send a copy to the planning officer as well. For example, if you have particular concerns about highway safety, it can pay dividends to ask an engineer from the highway authority to come out to the site so you can show him or her exactly what the problem is. Do not wait until the consultee has responded to the council, approach them as early in the application process as you can.

Remember this

You can directly contact the bodies and organizations the council consults on applications.

LOBBYING COUNCILLORS

Councils have guidelines on what forms and level of contact are appropriate with applicants and objectors. These vary between authorities. Before trying to make contact with a councillor(s), phone the department of the council which manages councillors and committee meetings and find out what the rules are in your district. Bear this in mind when deciding on whether and what approaches to make.

District councillors can bring influence to bear on planning officers. Where they disagree with an officer's opinion, usually, they are able to ask for an application to be decided by the planning committee, rather than by the planning officers. Council rules on the circumstances in which applications go to committee vary considerably. These rules are referred to as the council's delegation scheme. Generally, the larger and more contentious an application is, the more likely it is to be decided by the planning committee. With some councils, a given number of objections or the presence of a petition can automatically trigger a committee hearing. Be aware that some councils only allow councillors to call applications to committee at a relatively early stage in the application process.

Where an application scheme would genuinely be harmful to your home or business, councillors are likely to have some sympathy for your cause. Not all councillors sit on a planning committee. Approaching those who are on the committee is often most effective but other councillors can still influence applications and they are bound to have political friends and allies on the committee. Contact your local councillors, ideally by phone, explain that you are a local resident and find out if they are aware of the application in question. If they are, ask their opinion on it as this might help you to couch your concerns in terms likely to elicit their support or sympathy. As with planning officers, responses vary from the non-committal through to active support. Where relevant, invite the councillors to visit your property so they can view the potential impact and better understand your concerns. Do not bombard councillors with too much technical information, as they are laypeople and not professional planners. Although, strictly speaking, your personal circumstances should not influence planning decisions, they might help sway councillors towards your way of thinking. Be careful to ensure that the councillors grasp the fact that you have genuine planning concerns and that these are your prime motivation for objecting. Councillors can be a little circumspect in their reactions to an application, not wishing to be seen to be pre-judging the outcome prior to the committee meeting. Where an application is not going to committee, they can speak to planning officers, and it is not unknown for political pressure to bring about a change of heart in a planning officer.

Where an application is going to be decided by the planning committee, you can circulate information direct to some or all of the committee members in advance of the meeting, depending on the scale of the proposal and its effects. In cases of localized impact, it is sufficient to send material to the ward councillors and the chairperson. Resist supplying councillors with too much information. They are likely to have a number of applications to consider, so keep your representations to them short and to the point. Circulate information to councillors as a back up to attending and speaking at the committee, not in place of personal attendance, unless for some reason you are unable to attend and cannot get someone else to go in your place.

Remember this

You can lobby councillors who are highly influential in planning decisions.

ATTENDING AND SPEAKING AT COMMITTEE MEETINGS

Most councils allow objectors to speak at planning committees (see Chapter 4). Whether this is necessary or worthwhile depends to an extent on the officer's report, which will be published some days prior to the committee meeting (see Chapter 4). If the officer's report does not make the recommendation you hoped for or all the points you believe are pertinent, or where matters appear finely balanced, attending and speaking at committee gives your objection extra force. This could sway enough councillors to get the decision you want. Applications are decided by a vote and a simple majority prevails. Consequently, changing even one or two councillors' minds could make the difference between refusal and approval. Most committee decisions are made in line with the planning officer's recommendation but not all. Some planning committees are more inclined to go against an officer's advice than others. Going through the planning committee's minutes for one or two previous meetings (which you should find on the council's website) should indicate whether or not the committee is inclined to do its own thing. Attending a committee meeting beforehand can be educational as well, revealing particular issues of interest or concern to members. Attendance can also help you to identify which members tend to take a leading role in discussions and appear most influential over decisions. Those might be the members on whom your lobbying should be focused.

Key idea

Not all planning committee decisions follow the planning officer's advice.

You can find out when the committee meeting is to be held on the council's website, or by phoning the council, and then look out for the agenda being published before the meeting. Some councils automatically send out letters to everyone who has commented on an application, giving the date and location of the meeting and explaining the procedure. Most councils produce leaflets on attending and speaking at committee and these might be included with, or referred to, in the notification letter.

Ensure you know when you must register to speak as this can be several days before the meeting. It is rare to be able simply to turn up and talk. The number of speakers is usually limited and places might be allocated on a 'first come, first served' basis. Where many speakers are concerned about the same issues, councils often encourage one speaker to present the collective view. Parish councils are generally given an opportunity to speak, so if you have a locally contentious application, try to co-ordinate with both parish councillors and other objectors to make the most effective use of the time available.

Presentations are usually limited to two or three minutes. Many councils operate a 'traffic light' system where a green light indicates the start of your allotted time, orange indicates 30 seconds to go and red means stop. Most committee chairmen allow you to finish a sentence after your time is up, but in the interests of fairness, time limits are normally quite strictly enforced. Some councils allow councillors to ask speakers questions but never vice versa. Be warned that sitting through a committee discussion can be a frustrating experience because councillors might not address the issues you feel are vital and it can be clear that they have misunderstood aspects of the application.

When you attend a planning committee, check for any late amendments to the agenda or officers' reports. Arriving in good time gives you an opportunity to consider any late changes that might necessitate tweaking your speech.

Key idea

Most councils allow objectors to attend and speak at their planning committee meetings.

▶ Content of speech

What to say in your speech will be determined by the nature of your objections and how to frame these is covered in the next chapter. Writing down and reading out your speech helps cope with the strict time limit. What you might lose in spontaneity can be offset by ensuring you get your key points across. On the other hand, a less scripted delivery can be more compelling to listen to. Assuming you feel strongly about the development in question, try to convey some of that emotion to the members as this will grab their attention. Be aware, though, that expressing feelings out loud can heighten them, so do not put so much passion into your speech that you risk struggling to get through it. It is commonplace to see objectors run out of time before they deliver their concluding punchline. Two or three minutes is a very short period, so when you plan your speech, practise it aloud to ensure it fits into the allotted time. Do not waste time greeting the chairman and members of the committee, thanking them for the opportunity to speak or reciting your credentials. A brief 'good afternoon/evening' is adequate before getting straight into your points.

Planning committees can refuse applications or approve them, very likely subject to conditions. They can also defer a decision pending receipt of more information or amendments to a scheme, or to enable the whole committee to make a site visit. Make it clear in your speech which of these outcomes you are asking for.

INVOLVING YOUR MP

Taking your concerns about planning applications to your local MP is not usually as effective as you might think, and the support of an MP certainly doesn't trump planning considerations. Many MPs simply refer the matter back to the head of the planning department, who in turn shunts it on to the case officer. Except for major applications with a district-wide or regional significance, the most you might expect from your MP is a letter expressing sympathy for your concerns. Councillors are more likely to be influenced by an MP's involvement, but whether they support or reject his or her concerns might be determined more by political affiliation than anything else. Nevertheless, there is little to lose by writing to your MP or turning up at a surgery, if you feel your objections are falling on deaf ears at the council.

LOBBYING GOVERNMENT

Applications can be 'called-in' at any stage of the process, before the decision is taken, for determination by the Secretary of State for Communities and Local Government in England, and by Ministers in Scotland and Wales (see Chapter 4).

Although any application could be called-in, the power is used sparingly and generally only where an application raises matters of regional or national significance, is at odds with national planning policy guidance or involves matters of national security or foreign governments. If you think an application has sufficient significance beyond its local implications, and that the council might approve it, you can ask the government (in England, Scotland and Wales) to call-in the application. Called-in applications are then determined after a public inquiry.

If you are considering trying to get an application called-in, do not discuss this with the council, as it might speed up its consideration and grant permission before a call-in could take effect. If requesting a call-in, detail the application proposal and explain clearly why it is of such importance and why it should be taken out of the hands of the local council.

Remember this

It is possible to ask the government to decide certain applications rather than the council, via the 'call-in' procedure.

Focus points

* Object to planning applications that might harm your property.
* Report unlawful development.
* Observe the time limits for objecting.
* Lobby councillors.
* Attend and speak at the planning committee.

Next step

Having established where, when and how you can object to a planning application, appeal, or unauthorized development, you need to prepare your written objection, which is the vital element in influencing planning decisions.

Writing an
objection letter
or statement

In this chapter you will learn:

- ► *How to write an effective objection*
- ► *The importance of checking the facts*
- ► *What to look out for in the application forms and documents*
- ► *How to check the drawings*

Basis for effective objections

To be effective an objection should be made in writing, either in the form of a letter or a more formal statement that you submit in response to a planning application. Informal chats with planning officers, contact with councillors and speaking at planning committee are valuable additional ways to get your point across but all should be underpinned by a thorough, written objection. That objection forms part of the planning application file. It should be seen early on in the application process by the case officer, it is likely to be mentioned in the officer's report and, if the application is refused and an appeal results, it will be taken into account by the planning inspector deciding that appeal.

However outrageous a planning application might appear to be, make sure you get the facts before you dash off a letter of objection. Rumours about proposed development often circulate and local newspapers sometimes confuse the issue with inaccurate reporting. Unless you have been notified by letter or have seen a site notice, your first step should be to establish that there really is a formal planning application registered with the council. Do this by checking the council's online planning search facility, by phoning the planning department or by calling in at the council offices. Note the application reference number, or numbers, as there may be more than one application on the same property. For example, a development affecting a listed building would need an application for both listed building consent and planning permission. Also, developers sometimes submit more than one scheme for a site simultaneously, perhaps with a view to securing permission for something modest while pushing for a more adventurous scheme, which they will take to appeal if it is refused. Once you have the reference number, you can look up the details of the application and base your objection on the facts of the case. Representations based on a vague or mistaken understanding of what is actually proposed are not likely to be truly effective (see below).

Studying the application

Whether you are studying the application online or at the council offices, it is important to look at all the documents to be certain you fully understand what is proposed. The application forms are a good place to start as these give you a brief description of the proposed development as well as information on the main aspects of the proposal, including land ownership. There will also be a site location plan and, depending on the nature and complexity of the application, other drawings and supporting statements. This can amount to a great deal of information, so take notes as you work your way through. In particular, write down things you disagree with, anything you do not understand and points you need to check. Jot down planning policies the applicant is relying on where these are mentioned in an accompanying statement.

APPLICATION FORMS

These vary in content depending on the nature of the application. A householder application is a simplified version of a full application form. Listed building and Conservation Area consent forms provide more information on the impact of the development on them. The forms are the same for England and Wales. Those in Scotland are broadly similar. In Northern Ireland, a basic form is supplemented by additional forms for specific types of development. Read through all the application forms carefully and make notes as you go of key information and points you might want to make use of in your objection. The headings you are likely to encounter in a form, based on a full application in England and Wales, and the significance of the information entered under them, are as follows.

▶ **Applicant name, address and contact details**

The applicant is not necessarily the owner of the property but is the person making the application or in whose name it is made. The applicant could be an individual, couple or company and, if a company, it can be difficult to pin down who is actually behind an application. The planning system is not that concerned with the identity of the applicant, as any permission granted attaches to the application site rather than the person making the application. Applications are sometimes made in the name of a 'front' company or organization, in order to avoid adverse reactions which the identity of intended occupiers might generate.

▶ Agent

This might be a planning consultant, architect or other advisor who is handling the application on behalf of the applicant. All correspondence on the application to and from the council is with the agent, where one is appointed. Anybody can act as an agent and it does not necessarily follow that an agent has any particular knowledge of planning. The presence of an unqualified agent or the absence of an agent can mean that an application is poorly presented or ill-advised, although that is not necessarily the case. Use of a qualified agent does not mean the scheme is a reasonable one either.

▶ Description of the proposal

Descriptions vary greatly from terse, such as 'detached dwelling', through to an exhaustive list of every aspect of the proposal. A brief description also covers the associated works, so, in the case of an application for a 'single dwelling', the access, parking area, boundary fences and services connections would all be taken as read as part of the scheme. Check that the application description tallies with what is shown on the drawings and described in any accompanying statements.

▶ Site address

Not all sites have a specific address. The location of large-scale developments, for example, might be quite vague, 'land west of Station Road' for example. This can lead people potentially affected by a development not to realize it is close by. If you think a given address is misleading, bring this to the attention of the planning officer as quickly as possible in an effort to get it rectified.

Pre-application advice

If the applicant has sought advice from the council before making a formal application, a summary of that advice should be set out on the form. Whether that advice appears positive or negative gives you an idea of the possible reaction of the planning officers to the formal application. Applicants might, however, put a positive spin on the advice they have been given or only quote selective parts which appear favourable. Councils are not bound by pre-application advice so do not assume that the decision on the formal application will automatically follow whatever was indicated in pre-application advice. The scheme might have been amended to reflect negative pre-application comments or an initially positive pre-application response could be reversed should planning problems come to light during consultations.

Access

Where a new access is sought or an existing access is to be altered or closed, this can affect highway safety as well as having visual impact, and may give rise to noise or disturbance for neighbours. New estate roads or the closure of existing roads can change traffic levels and flows, with implications for congestion, highway safety and the amenities of those living nearby. Judging whether an access would be safe involves looking for hazards in the vicinity, for example, junctions, pedestrian crossings, speed of traffic and obstructions to clear lines of visibility up and down the road. Inadequate or dangerous access is a common reason for refusal of planning applications, so consider this carefully and discuss any concerns you have with the planning officer and the highway officer.

Waste storage

All development generating waste should include suitable arrangements for its storage. This could be a significant planning consideration for larger commercial or industrial schemes as well as in smaller residential development where, on a constrained site, it can be difficult to achieve. The storage and removal of waste can involve noise, smells and heavy vehicle movements. Even a modest proposal, such as conversion of space over a shop into a flat, could harm neighbours if bin storage is not sensibly located and properly managed. If you are concerned about the adequacy of waste storage, speak to the waste disposal section of the council before taking the matter up with the planning officer.

▶ Authority employee/member

Where employees or members of the council, or their relatives, make applications, this must be flagged up on the form. Where such a relationship exists, extra vigilance is needed to ensure the application does not receive any special treatment and there is no bias in the decision.

▶ Materials

Choice of external finishes has a major bearing on the appearance of a building. Think about whether specified materials and colours are appropriate and check that what is written on the forms tallies with what is shown on the drawings. These details are particularly important where listed buildings and Conservation Areas are involved. It is common for the specification of external materials and finishes not to be pinned down until after permission is granted, by means of a condition requiring subsequent approval by the council. If you think that materials are central to the question of whether permission should be granted, take this up with the planning officer, who could ask the applicant for that information prior to making a decision on the application.

▶ Vehicle parking

The amount of parking for various types of vehicles gives a good idea of likely traffic flows to and from the site. Where existing parking numbers are given, you can check on site that these are accurate. Proposed parking spaces can be compared with the council's parking standards. The location of parking spaces can be significant too, as starting and manoeuvring vehicles are relatively noisy and can produce more in the way of fumes than cars passing in the street. Look at the plans to see if the parking spaces and turning areas are workable and of adequate size and whether there would be adverse effects on your property. If in doubt, check technical requirements with the highway authority.

▶ Foul sewage

While most new development connects to a public sewer, it does not follow that the sewer has adequate capacity. Developers might simply tick the 'mains sewer' box without actually knowing whether there is one, where it is or its capacity. Connections to sewers that involve crossing land outside the applicant's ownership or control might not be achievable without the landowner's consent. Private systems require space, somewhere to discharge excess water and access for maintenance, so check the application plans to ensure what is shown is consistent with the forms and does not impinge on land outside the applicant's control. If you are aware of any particular problems with drainage in the near vicinity, discuss this with the body responsible for drainage and/or bring these to the planning officer's attention.

▶ Flood risk

See what the applicants say about flood risk, proximity to rivers and streams and whether the proposal might increase flood risk elsewhere. Maps, which are accessible on the Environment Agency website (refer to the equivalent bodies in Scotland and Northern Ireland), show the extent of areas at risk of flooding so you can verify this yourself, if you doubt what the applicant has said. Local knowledge can be helpful in identifying potential problems that applicants might not know about or be hoping to gloss over.

Surface water disposal, the run-off from roofs and hard surfaces, can have implications for local flooding. Where soakaways are suggested as a convenient solution, what you might know about soil conditions in the area can indicate whether they would work. In heavy clay soils, for example, they generally do not. Discharge into ditches and streams might need to be moderated by a holding pond or tank, to avoid flash flooding at times of intense rainfall. Local residents' experience of such problems can be invaluable in ensuring that new development does not make them worse.

▶ Biodiversity and geological conservation

The presence of protected species on or near a site can be a significant constraint on development. Applicants might wish to avoid admitting the existence of such species because of the cost and delay of surveys and mitigation of any possible harm. What local people know about a site or area can be drawn upon to ascertain whether this part of the form has been completed accurately. Tell the planning officer about any inaccuracies or omissions so that the applicant can be requested to commission appropriate investigation. Where protected species are noted as being present on the site, the application should be accompanied by a survey. Study this to ascertain whether its findings tally with your knowledge of the site and surroundings.

▶ Existing use

The existing lawful use of a site is an important base point from which to judge the impact of any proposed use. Check the existing use is correctly described and not exaggerated to lessen the apparent impact of the proposed use. This section of the form also covers contamination. Your knowledge of the past uses of a site can show whether answers given here are accurate. The possible presence of contamination generally triggers the need for an environmental survey and mitigation works. This adds cost to an application scheme which applicants might seek to avoid. Take up concerns about contamination with the planning officer but also speak to the council's environmental health department, as those officers are likely to be consulted on the matter by the planning officer.

▶ Trees and hedges

Trees and hedges can be harmed by building works either directly, in that they have to be removed, or indirectly, by excavation and work close to them. Where either applies, a full tree survey should be included in the application. Applicants might try to avoid the expense of a survey and any hint that there could be a problem by ticking the 'no' boxes in respect of the presence and significance of trees in and around the site. If there are trees on or close to the site, ensure they are shown accurately on the application plans and are properly accounted for in a survey. Find out whether any trees are subject to a tree preservation order as this would strengthen your case where you are worried about their potential loss. If there are trees that are particularly special, either as individual specimens or in terms of their contribution to the appearance or character of the area, ask the council's tree officer to consider imposing a tree preservation order.

▶ Trade effluent

This section not only alerts to you any potentially toxic effluent that could be a concern, but also enables you to judge the impact of vehicle movements required to remove it.

▶ Residential units

Where new housing is proposed, it should be evident from the description of the proposal what is being planned. The answers to this question, though, give a handy breakdown of the number, size and likely tenure of the units which is particularly helpful for assessing larger-scale proposals. You can, for example, gauge whether proposed house types would meet the needs of the area.

▶ Non-residential floor space

For commercial and other proposals, this table gives a helpful breakdown of the floor areas of the different uses in a scheme and identifies any changes in the amount of each use. This highlights points such as likely levels of activity and any loss of protected uses.

▶ Employment

The level of employment gives an indication of both the general level of activity arising from a proposal and the likely level of traffic generation. Creation of employment can be regarded as a major benefit of development. Where that might be the case, look carefully at whether the projected number of jobs to be created appears realistic.

▶ Hours of opening

The application form allows opening hours to be recorded or a simple 'not known' box to be ticked. Where opening hours could be significant, in terms of noise or disturbance, request in your objection that, should permission be granted, they are controlled by a specific condition.

▶ Site area

This should be the area of the red-lined site on the location plan. It is used in calculating outline application fees, in situations where the density of development might be an issue and can trigger certain policies, including affordable housing requirements. In the latter case, it might be desirable to ensure any density calculations are correct and you can calculate the site area yourself from the scale location or site plan.

▶ Industrial or commercial processes and machinery

This section concerns proposed activities and all plant and machinery involved, including ventilation and air conditioning. Applicants can try to avoid details that might be damaging to their case by answering 'not known'. If in doubt about technical information given, seek confirmation from the planning officer as to precisely what the nature and implications of any processes or machinery might be. If machinery could cause noise, vibration or smells, raise this in your objection and seek reassurances that full details of likely impacts are ascertained and assessed by the council, or would be controlled via conditions. Extract systems serving restaurants and take-away kitchens are a frequent cause of nuisance, as are systems serving car spraying workshops.

▶ Hazardous substances

Where a proposal involves hazardous waste, expect the council to impose conditions on the grant of planning permission to make sure such waste is disposed of safely. Waste disposal also has implications for traffic generation which you need to take into account.

▶ Site visit

This question aims to establish whether the site is visible from a public place, such as an adjoining road or footpath or, if not, with whom arrangements for a site visit should be made. If you think a planning officer needs to go onto the site to assess its impact fully, or you want the case officer to visit you to assess likely impacts on your property, contact the officer early in the application process to make these requests.

▶ Certificates

All applications must be accompanied by a certificate stating whether the applicant owns all of the application site – that is, the area shown edged in red on the site plan. If not, a formal notice must be served on the owner saying what has been applied for. Where any owners are not known and cannot be found, the application must be advertised in a local newspaper. Applicants must also certify whether the site forms part of an agricultural holding. If so, a notice has to be served on any agricultural tenants. These notices are important because they alert owners or agricultural tenants to any application on land they own or farm.

Remember this

Study planning application forms carefully and cross-check the information against the plans and any accompanying statements.

APPLICATION DRAWINGS

First, distinguish between the formal drawings drawn to scale on which any planning permission would be based and any illustrative drawings. The latter have no formal status and can show beguiling impressions of what a proposed development might look like that are far removed from reality. The formal drawings comprise a site location plan; existing and proposed site layout or block plans, showing the existing and intended layout; floor plans; and elevations, showing the proposed building from all sides. There may also be a roof plan and cross-section drawings through the building and/or the site, where there are changes in land level.

Start by looking at the location plan. This is based on an Ordnance Survey map and shows the extent of the application site edged with a red line, and any other adjoining land in the applicant's ownership or control edged with a blue line. Check that the plan is accurate and, importantly, up to date. Applicants sometimes use old plans that might not show recently constructed buildings, extensions or other changes to the surroundings. If you share a boundary with an application site, make sure that boundary is shown accurately and does not accidentally include part of your property.

Similarly, examine existing and proposed site plans for accuracy, ensuring that all man-made and natural features are accurately shown. Buildings, access drives, parking areas, boundaries and services should all be shown, where relevant, together with trees, hedges and any open or uncultivated areas. Proposed site plans should indicate how the whole site is to be developed, including what is to be done with parts of it not directly affected by the development. If your property adjoins the site, look to see whether any changes to the boundary wall, fence or hedge are proposed. Where you own these, any proposed changes might need your consent, and there may be legal implications to discuss with the applicant. This would not be a planning matter but the fact that the applicant does not have control over the boundary could have planning consequences.

Elevations should show materials and finishes so that a clear impression can be gained of what the building would look like. Floor plans detail how the accommodation would be laid out internally. Where there are changes in levels, cross-section drawings should show these and how a building would sit relative to the natural ground level. Check these drawings individually but also look at them together to ensure they are consistent. For example, a window or door position shown on a floor plan should match exactly the position on the relevant elevation drawing. Discrepancies between drawings can lead to confusion over what is actually permitted, if permission is granted. Do not just rely on the planning officers to pick up these errors as they might let them slip through the net.

If you are checking measurements on a paper drawing, make sure the copy you are looking at has been printed at the correct scale. Drawings that are scanned then printed can suffer scale distortions. Drawings should have a scale bar marked on them, which you can use to make certain the scale is accurate. Do not try to scale from a computer screen unless the council's website has a scaling facility.

ACCOMPANYING STATEMENTS
As a rule, the larger and more complex an application scheme is, the more reports, statements and technical information accompany it. Some statements, such as a design and access statement, should be readily understandable, while others, like acoustic and environmental contamination reports, can be full of jargon and figures impenetrable to a layperson. All technical reports should, though, have a summary or conclusions that are more intelligible. Despite their technical nature, it is worth reading through these reports to ensure that basic facts about the site and its surroundings are accurately reflected. It would be rare for a technical report to be prepared by someone living close to the site and basic errors can creep in that distort the findings. Also, see when the report was prepared, as it might be out of date. For example, a highway safety report might be based on year-old accident records and have missed recent incidents.

PLANNING HISTORY

While looking at an application online or at the council's offices, find out whether the site has any planning history. Past applications are a useful source of information, especially if they are for something similar to the current application. Past refusals of applications and dismissed appeals give you in-depth information on what the council's or appeal inspector's concerns were and which policies were central to the decisions. If permission has been granted in the past for the same type of development as the current proposal, which was never implemented, think about what might have changed since that decision, which could now point to a different outcome. Policies at all levels change over time, so just because something was found to be compliant with policy a few years ago does not automatically mean it will be now. Your local knowledge of any physical changes in the vicinity since an earlier decision could be an important part of your objection.

CHECKING FACTS

It is essential that any objection to a planning application is based on an accurate understanding of precisely what is proposed. An objection based on an incorrect understanding of a proposed development risks having its credibility and influence undermined. Where possible, study the application forms, drawings and documents yourself, rather than relying on hearsay. Where any aspect of the application is unclear, speak to the planning officer and seek clarification. Some drawings of complex-shaped buildings can be difficult to interpret, and calling in at the council's offices to get a planning officer to talk you through them is often the best way forward.

Once you have ascertained exactly what is proposed, you need to establish what effects the development would have. Again, this analysis should be as factual as possible, as facts are infinitely more compelling than assertions. If you believe a scheme would cause highway safety problems, for example, seek information from the local police on accident records, rather than simply stating 'the road is dangerous'. However well you know the site and its surroundings, look at it afresh, with the application drawings in hand, to be clear that your understanding of how it might work or what it might look like is correct. Walk the area and try to visualize the completed development in place. Where would it be seen from and what would it look like? How would it relate to neighbouring buildings and to its surroundings? If you are concerned about loss of privacy, consider the position of and likely views from windows and note which rooms they would serve. If you anticipate overshadowing or loss of light, see where the sun rises and sets at different times of the year, whether anything currently obscures it, such as trees or existing buildings, and what might change were the development to go ahead. Take into account any proposals to mitigate possible harm, such as hard or soft landscaping schemes, obscure-glazing in windows or the removal of something that is currently an eyesore or nuisance. An objective assessment of the likely success of such measures can affect the credibility of your case.

Remember this

Base your objection on the facts of the case taken from the application forms, drawings and statements.

Planning policy

Once you fully understand the nature of the proposal and its likely impact, it is highly desirable to relate your findings to planning policy. There is no doubt that an objection which simply alerts a planning officer to problems with a development is much better than no objection at all. That said, an objection which not only points out defects but identifies how those defects run counter to planning policy is likely to be more influential.

To find out which local planning policies are relevant to a particular development, ask the council which policy documents are currently used as the basis for planning decisions. Planning policy documents and the policies they contain are described in Chapter 2. It might be clear from the council's website, but a call to the planning policy section is still a worthwhile precaution as policies frequently change. Once you have the correct policy document, look for the policies that are most applicable to the proposal in hand. Do not go for an exhaustive list of every policy that might be remotely relevant. A clear conflict with just one or two policies might well be enough to justify refusing an application. If it is not obvious which policies might be applicable, phone the application case officer or duty planning officer to ask them. Alternatively, visiting the duty planning officer at the council's offices should provide clarification.

Establish whether there are any supplementary guidance documents pertinent to the development. These can give considerable detail against which you can judge the application. For example, many councils have comprehensive guidance on house extensions, some with diagrams illustrating the sorts of design approaches to various forms of extension that might be acceptable and those that are unlikely to be. This sort of guidance can be particularly helpful where you are criticizing a subjective aspect of development, like design.

Where applications are accompanied by design and access or planning statements, these documents should contain references to policies with which the applicant is claiming compliance. Research these and take them into account. Refute such claims if you disagree with them.

It is also worthwhile considering national policy guidance. At the time of writing, in England the National Planning Policy Framework (NPPF) is relatively succinct at 50-odd pages divided into 13 sections. It is not too arduous a task to find guidance relevant to most development proposals. Scotland's National Planning Framework is a considerably longer document but, with a detailed index, it is reasonably easy to navigate. Planning Policy Wales' document is of a similar length, but is also supplemented by some 22 Technical Advice Notes. In Northern Ireland there remain more than 20 Planning Policy Statements each covering particular topics. Bear in mind that local policies should be in line with national policy but there can be differences in emphasis and interpretation. This is particularly true of England's NPPF where the brevity of some of the guidance leaves much to be interpreted locally.

Material considerations

In addition to analysing policy, consider what, if any, material considerations might be relevant. Review the list in Chapter 3 and see whether there are material considerations present that are not addressed directly by the planning policies you have identified. Compare your analysis of the application, and your concerns, with the list of factors in Chapter 3 that are not usually taken into account, to be certain your points are all valid planning matters. Be objective about what is likely to be considered relevant or important. It is not uncommon for objection letters to reveal that the objector has a particular bee in his or her bonnet about some issue which is not of general concern or of great relevance to a decision. This not only undermines the objection but deflects from other, potentially more compelling arguments.

Remember that private legal matters, such as rights of way and restrictive covenants should not be of concern to the council, nor should they influence a planning decision. If there is a potential private legal matter, do not rely on it in your objection and keep in mind that the grant of planning permission would not override any legal restrictions.

Objection statement

There are no hard and fast rules about how to structure an objection statement or letter. Statements should be clear and concise. Ideally, type out your objection or, if handwritten, make sure it is clearly legible. A truly effective statement should do the following:

- ▶ identify the application reference and site address;

- ▶ state who is objecting and their relationship to the development (ie neighbour, local resident, etc.);

- ▶ identify the key points of objection and who or what would be affected;

- ▶ provide evidence to back up those points;

- ▶ link the objection points to relevant policy and highlight conflicts;

- ▶ where you believe defects could be overcome, suggest conditions or amendments to the scheme; otherwise, conclude that the application should be refused.

When quoting planning policies, it is not generally necessary to write out the whole policy, just give the policy reference. That said, there may be particular passages of policy wording to which you want to draw attention, so by all means include them.

Illustrating your objection with photographs or drawings can be effective in making points but make certain they are fair representations, for example do not use the zoom facility on a camera to exaggerate the proximity or prominence of a building and do not take photographs from improbable angles, such as from up a ladder or tree.

If you suspect there is a technical problem with the application, such as the certificate of ownership has been incorrectly filled in or perhaps the wrong application procedure has been adopted, take this up with the planning officer. Mention technical issues but appreciate they can usually be resolved, so keep your written objection focused mainly on the planning issues.

There are innumerable reasons why you might want to object to a planning application which affects your or your community's interests. Generally, problems likely to arise from a proposed development have to be significant – or 'material' in

Table 12.1 Examples of planning issues that can result in refusal

Domestic extensions, houses in gardens and demolition and rebuild of dwellings

Overlooking of windows of habitable rooms and private rear garden areas

Overbearing, loss of light and outlook

Excessive height, bulk or scale

Building too close to neighbours' boundaries, over-development

Loss of trees, building too close to trees

Design, materials, finishes out of keeping with original or adjoining building

Inadequate access, turning or parking space

Out of character with neighbouring properties or surrounding area

Town centre developments and changes of use

Incompatibility with neighbouring uses

Loss of retail or business uses

Inadequate parking

Incompatible urban design

Inadequate waste disposal facilities

Noise and disturbance, unsocial opening hours

Over-concentration of one use in an area (restaurants, clubs, student accommodation)

New housing estates or business areas

Adequate allocation of housing/business space elsewhere

Erosion of countryside, loss of open space

Highway safety, traffic generation

Lack of, or distance from, public transport and facilities

Incompatible with amenities of adjoining residentsImpact on wildlife habitats and protected species

Rural development

Unsustainable, remote location

Highway safety and inadequacy of road network

Loss of rural businesses or facilities such as village shops and pubs

Loss of trees and harm to landscape

Flood risk

Contaminated site

Loss of high quality agricultural land

planning jargon – in order for them to be reasons for refusing planning permission. Some factors result in refusal of planning permission more often than others. Table 12.1 sets out various forms of development and the most common objections that lead to refusal. In specially designated areas, anything that conflicts with the purposes behind the designation is likely to be a particularly compelling ground for objection. For example, in Conservation Areas, harm to the historic character and appearance of the area is likely to result in refusal of permission. Similarly, in an Area of Outstanding Natural Beauty, harm to the natural landscape will probably not be tolerated. In Green Belt anything that impacts on the openness of the area is likely to be rejected.

Examples of effective objection letters are set out in Figures 12.1 and 12.2. Figure 12.1 is an example of an objection letter in response to a poorly thought-through neighbours' house extension. The issues are not complex and a formal statement is not necessary. The letter clearly identifies the cause of the problem (the blank side wall) and its relationship to the objector's property. It then sets out the issues that would arise if the wall was built and goes on to show how those issues conflict with specific criteria in local planning policy. The invitation to the planning officer to visit provides contact details. The objection ends with confirmation that an alternative solution might be more acceptable. This is helpful to the planning officer but could also ease any friction with the neighbour that might arise from the objection.

Figure 12.2 is a more formal objection letter, dealing with a larger-scale housing development that has implications beyond the objector's home. Numbered paragraphs and headings give the objection structure and identify clearly the main issues. The letter is careful to avoid, bar one brief mention, repeated reference to the objector's own amenities, views or opinions because the issues go beyond the objector's rear garden and personal interests. A recent appeal decision is quoted as helpful evidence in support of highway safety concerns.

Director of Planning
Belvedere District Council

Dear Sir/Madam

PLANNING APPLICATION REFERENCE AD/2678/HH
27 LOWER STREET, BOSTOCK HEATH

I wish to register an objection to this application for a side and rear extension to 27 Lower Street. I am the owner of, and live at 29 Lower Street, the adjoining dwelling to the north of 27.

The proposed two-storey side and rear extension would result in the north flank wall of 27 extending to within 1 metre of our mutual boundary and 4 metres west, beyond our rear wall. The tall, blank side wall will block light from the only window of our kitchen on the south side of our house and our rear conservatory, both of which currently enjoy good light levels and an open outlook. The proposed flank wall would be overbearing and create an oppressive sense of enclosure.

I am aware that policy RES 6 of the Local Plan requires residential extensions to preserve the amenities of neighbours in respect of natural light (criterion b) and outlook (criterion c). There is a clear conflict with policy here as the adverse effect of this proposal on my amenities would be severe. This could best be appreciated by the case officer visiting my property to view the situation from inside my house. I can be contacted at any time on 07911 123654 to arrange a mutually convenient time for the officer to call in.

Finally, I should add that I am not averse to my neighbours building an extension but feel a design could be devised that meets their needs while avoiding the severe impacts on my amenities which the current proposal threatens.

Yours faithfully

Figure 12.1 Sample objection letter to a neighbour's extension

Head of Planning
Chelsfold Borough Council

Dear Sir/Madam

PLANNING APPLICATION REFERENCE AD/2679/FUL
LAND SOUTH OF MILL LANE, BREYTON

Proposed development of 75 houses

I live at No 20 Pond Lane and my rear garden would adjoin
the east boundary of the site. I wish to register my objection
to this application for the following reasons:

Planning principle

The site lies outside the development boundary of Breyton
and is in a designated countryside area where policy H2 of the
Local Plan indicates that residential development will only be
permitted in exceptional circumstances, none of which apply
here. Previous applications to develop the land in 2001, 2006
and 2010 have been refused. The NPPF has come into force
since the last application and this encourages development in
sustainable locations. This site is over 0.8 km from the nearest
bus route, and the shops and other facilities of the town
centre are over 2 km away.

Site layout

The site layout would be cramped and out of keeping with
the lower-density housing in this edge-of-town location. On
the east side of the site, the proposed houses would be close
to the boundary and would overlook the rear gardens and
rear windows of adjoining houses in Pond Lane. In addition,
in places, including adjoining my house, the 'rear garage court'
arrangement would bring parking and manoeuvring vehicles
right up to the boundary of the relatively short rear gardens of
the Pond Lane houses. One of the attractions of the Pond Lane

Figure 12.2 Sample objection letter to a large-scale housing development

houses is their open westerly aspect, with most of the houses having patios or terraces providing outdoor seating where the evenings can be enjoyed in summer. This amenity would be destroyed by the immediate proximity of a garage court. The proposal, therefore, would fail to protect the amenities of neighbouring properties, contrary to criterion b of Local Plan policy H4, and the cramped layout would conflict with design policy DS2.

The site has a number of mature oak trees along the southern boundary. These are not shown on the layout plan and do not appear to have been taken into account in the layout.

Setting of listed building

The Grade II listed Manor House adjoins the western boundary of the site. At present there are public views of the house across the northern part of the site from Mill Lane. The house is a well known local historic landmark and the proposed development, with close-knit housing across the Mill Lane frontage, would block those views and harm the currently open setting of the house. This would not comply with Local Plan policy BE6.

Traffic generation

Mill Lane already suffers from congestion which would be exacerbated by the additional traffic from 75 homes. The lane is narrow to the east and, with only an informal and narrow footpath, such additional traffic would be a danger to pedestrians and act as a further discouragement to walking and cycling to the town centre. A recent appeal at 25 Mill Road (ref APP/2013/S/723175), concerning four new houses, was dismissed on highway safety grounds. Although the principal issue was poor visibility, the Inspector commented that additional traffic on Mill Lane would have an unacceptable impact on highway safety (paragraph 8).

Figure 12.2 (*Continued*)

Conclusions

The proposed development clearly conflicts with a number of Local Plan policies and the principle of developing this site would be at odds with the thrust of NPPF towards sustainable development. The layout would be cramped and out of character and would compromise the amenities of neighbours. It fails to take into account the setting of the listed Manor House and ignores the presence of significant trees. Existing traffic problems would be made worse and pedestrian safety compromised. Consequently, this application should be refused.

Yours faithfully

Figure 12.2 (Continued)

TONE FOR OBJECTIONS

It is important to get the tone of your objection right, so that it carries the maximum authority and influence. A letter full of capitalized words, underlining and exclamation marks suggests an emotional response rather than one based on facts and careful assessment. A measured tone is the one to aim for, where the strength of the facts and arguments make a compelling case with which any reasonable person would have to agree. Be careful not to exaggerate or to make unsubstantiated claims. Bear in mind that your particular likes, dislikes and priorities might not be shared by everyone. Planners assess applications against a general yardstick of what the average person might find acceptable, so try to broaden your points beyond your own personal interests. Do not criticize the applicant or the council, and especially not the planning officer, whose co-operation you are trying to foster.

Remember this

Adopt a measured tone for your objection and avoid an emotion-based response.

Using precedents

Precedents – past approvals and refusals of permission –
and the fear of setting a poor precedent are often quoted in
support of objections. Care needs to be taken with precedents,
to ensure they are genuinely comparable to the proposal in
question and that the planning decisions were taken in light
of the same policies which apply now. Every application is
supposed to be decided on its merits and it is rare for planning
applications involving different properties to be identical in all
respects. If you think there are useful precedents applicable to
your objection, do not rely solely on them, rather, use them to
support your key planning arguments.

There is no harm in using the fear of setting an undesirable
precedent as an argument but, again, it should support
substantial planning arguments. If you can show that a
particular development would be genuinely harmful, then it
goes without saying that it would not be something that should
be repeated elsewhere. Identifying specific situations where a
certain form of development could be repeated is more effective
than a general and, therefore, vague assertion that a precedent
would be harmful.

One form of precedent worth careful consideration is appeal
decisions, especially recent ones that dealt with either sites or
issues similar to the one you are objecting to. Councils do not
like having their decisions overturned at appeal and usually
pay attention to what appeal inspectors say in their decision
letters. If you quote from an appeal decision, give the address
of the property concerned and the appeal reference. As with
any precedent, do not rely entirely on what an inspector has
said elsewhere. Set out your arguments and evidence, and then
demonstrate how the appeal decision supports your position.

Focus points

* Study application forms, drawings and documents.
* Check the facts.
* Look up and refer to relevant planning policy in your objection.
* Make your objection concise and structured, and adopt a measured tone.
* Use precedents which are directly comparable.

Next step

Once you understand exactly what is being proposed and have thought through your grounds for objection, consider whether your position would be strengthened by mobilizing support from others and raising the profile of your campaign.

Mobilizing support

In this chapter you will learn:

- ▶ *Why it is important to decide whether to seek support and, if so, how much support you might need*
- ▶ *The various ways in which you can gain support from the wider community*

Considering whether and how much support is necessary

Mobilizing others to object to a planning application can greatly improve your chances of getting an application refused. This applies regardless of whether the application is for something quite small-scale, which only affects a very few people, or something with implications for a whole community. In the former case, it might just be a question of getting your near neighbours on board, in the latter, a much broader strategy needs to be adopted. Keep in mind that a large number of people with a poorly articulated objection is likely to be less effective than a few backing well thought-out arguments. Parish and district councillors do, though, respond to weight of numbers; after all, those objectors are the same people who vote the councillors into office. Applications refused by councillors on flimsy grounds supported by large numbers of objectors tend to get approved at appeal, where the influence of local politics is much less significant. One of the criteria for determining the method of appeal (written representations, hearing of public inquiry) is whether the proposal has generated significant local interest. Locally contentious applications are more likely to be considered by a hearing or inquiry. Both add time and cost to the appeal process, factors that could deter an applicant from appealing.

Before you rush to mobilize support, maybe canvass the opinions of friends and family. Is this really an issue likely to be of wider interest? If a development would only affect your property and no one else's, the planning officer is going to be primarily interested in your amenities and opinion. Getting others to support your case might help raise its profile but the key consideration would remain the impact on you and your house.

Key idea

A few people making good planning points is better than a lot of people making poor ones.

Gaining support

APPROACHING NEIGHBOURS

Local issues have the potential to be divisive so, if you try to mobilize neighbours, be extra careful to identify genuine problems or harm that might arise from an application. Avoid questioning the motives, taste or sanity of the applicants; the person whose support you are trying to foster might be their close friend, business colleague or even a relative.

How you approach neighbours is a matter of personal choice but, whether it is via phone, email, note through their letter box, social media or knocking on their doors, a series of questions might well be the most effective strategy. Are they aware of the application? Have they thought of the harmful implications you have identified? If they are concerned about those harmful implications, would they join you in seeking either amendments to the proposal or its refusal? Avoid putting neighbours in a position where they feel they are being pushed into taking action, as they might react against that pressure.

When mobilizing neighbours, make sure you are clear about what you want them to do. Tell neighbours when objections have to be made, how to make them and give them the planning application reference and correct site address. You could suggest that, as well as sending a written objection to the council, they contact their local councillor to apply pressure there (having first established the council's lobbying rules as described in Chapter 11). Again, provide contact details. The easier it is for neighbours to get involved, the more likely it is they will do so. It might be tempting to provide neighbours with a standard letter for them to use as a template for their objections. This tends to dilute the message, as lots of letters all saying exactly the same thing suggests an orchestrated campaign rather than necessarily genuine concern from a large sector of the community. By all means point out the key problems you think the development will create but urge individuals to voice their concerns in their own words. If necessary, you could help by taking a note of neighbours' points and writing tailored letters on their behalf for them to sign.

Remember this

Give neighbours all the information they need but avoid providing template letters.

RAISING A PETITION

Going door to door with a petition and leaving copies in local shops and with local businesses can elicit a lot of signatures. For optimum effect, a petition should clearly state the planning objections to the application, not simply say that the undersigned are opposed to it. The latter would carry little weight with planning officers, although an impressive number of signatures would be likely to focus councillors' attention, regardless of what was actually signed. A few councils automatically consider applications at planning committee where a petition of a prescribed number of signatures is submitted. Check with the council whether that is the case in your area.

Signatures on a petition are not generally as effective as individual letters of objection. In some cases, a petition organized by a lone but very keen objector, merely serves to emphasize that it is one individual's personal campaign, rather than necessarily indicative of a wider concern within the community. Where a number of individuals are writing letters of objection, a petition can add useful weight to those objections.

GETTING PUBLICITY

There are numerous ways of publicizing your campaign but, before you rush to do so, consider what effect publicity might have on both those promoting the development and any members of the public supporting it. Your efforts to promote the arguments against a development could lead to increased efforts by those in favour. Getting attention for your cause can include:

- leaflets
- posters and balloons
- T-shirts, caps and badges

- public meetings (see below)
- websites
- social media and email
- newspapers, local and national
- local radio
- demonstrations

It is worth bearing in mind that greater public awareness can attract media interest and there is a risk that this can result in publicity that is either factually inaccurate or 'spun' to make it more interesting or controversial than it really is. One way to try to reduce this risk is to issue a press release with a brief, clear and simple explanation of the facts and issues.

Key idea

A press release can prevent inaccurate media reporting.

Social media is a quick and cheap way of getting a message around your social circle and out into the public domain. Be conscious of the demographics of potential objectors and users of social media, as you might not be able to rely on this method alone to spread the word. For a large campaign, consider setting up a dedicated website or social media page where information, news, meetings and so on can be posted.

Campaign materials with a catchy slogan and/or logo printed on them can be produced at relatively low cost. Bright colours and distinctive design help gain attention, but also create an identity which adds credibility to the campaign.

HOLDING A PUBLIC MEETING

Where a proposed development is likely to harm a significant number of local residents, it often makes sense to try to motivate and co-ordinate objections by holding a meeting. This could be anything from an informal gathering of neighbours in your house, through to a larger-scale public meeting held in a local hall. Where a planning application is up and running, there is a balance to be struck between giving people adequate warning of the impending meeting and ensuring there is time to get objections in to the council in good time. It is usually worth inviting a parish council representative and your local district councillor. Consider inviting the local press and notifying local radio and television stations.

A public meeting is a good opportunity to canvass residents for skills and contacts that might be beneficial to the campaign. A broad cross-section of a community might well contain individuals with relevant professional, marketing or campaigning skills. There may be people with contacts on the parish or district council or relevant consultees, who might be able to speak to the individuals concerned.

Public meetings need some structure or else they risk becoming just a platform for a few vocal individuals to air their grievances. Prepare an agenda in advance and be certain to have someone chair the meeting who can keep control and work through the points methodically. Typical agenda topics might include:

- outline of the proposal and perceived problems

- brief review of local opinions

- overview of the application process

- further or detailed investigations needed

- scope for mitigation of harm

- canvassing of skills, contacts and resources

- whether to engage professional help

- fundraising

- getting publicity

- how and when to lodge objections

- lobbying of local councillors

- attendance at planning committee

- next steps or next meeting

During your meeting, circulate an attendance list to collect names, addresses and contact information. Also, have someone minute the proceedings and circulate those minutes, or a summary of them, to attendees afterwards. Where the scale justifies it, ask for contributions towards the cost of hiring the hall and any other campaign expenses. Be transparent about where any money collected is to be spent and what will happen if there is any surplus. Donating small left-over sums to charity, and being seen to make the donation, might be the most prudent way to address this.

Remember this

Prepare an agenda for your campaign meeting and ensure you stick to it.

For developments provoking wider interest in the community, or involving complicated issues, it is worth considering whether to get professional help from a planning consultant. Professional fees split between a number of people reduces their burden considerably. Help could be anything from general guidance on policy and principal issues, through to producing a formal objection statement and presenting the objection at planning committee. A planning consultant could also speak at your meeting, to make sure he or she fully understands the community's concerns and directs the campaign to the key planning issues and relevant policies.

SPECIAL INTEREST GROUPS

Special interest groups tend to monitor planning applications and respond to those that impact on their area of interest. For example, you would expect any significant development affecting wetlands to attract the attention of the RSPB. Such groups can add resources, specialist know-how and authority to an objection. Do not assume special interest groups are aware of every application relevant to their concerns. Contact them early in the application process to elicit their help. Give them all the relevant information about the application and any local knowledge you have about likely impacts on their area of interest.

Focus points

✳ Gain support from neighbours.
✳ Raise a petition.
✳ Alert the media.
✳ Hold a public meeting.
✳ Contact special interest groups.

→ Next step

If, despite your best efforts, the application to which you have objected is approved, there are still opportunities to influence the development to protect your interests. Where permission is refused you still need to be alert for an appeal or for an appeal against enforcement action taken to stop unlawful development. Chapter 14 deals with these further opportunities to protect your property.

After a decision

In this chapter you will learn:

- ▶ *What actions you can take, even after planning permission has been granted*
- ▶ *What to do in the event of an appeal*

Permission granted

When a development is permitted, there are various actions you can take to minimize its impact on your property. First, check what conditions have been imposed; some might require further approvals from the council before works commence and others, before the development is occupied. Particularly where the terms of the conditions are designed to protect neighbours or other amenities, keep an eye on the applicant's compliance with them. Some councils post on their website the drawings and information submitted to satisfy conditions, alongside planning application records. Others do not and you might have to speak to the planning officer or call in at the council offices to view details submitted to satisfy conditions.

There is nothing to prevent you contacting the planning officer to comment on submissions required by conditions, although there is no formal mechanism for members of the public to be involved. For example, a condition might require a landscaping scheme to be approved before work begins. You might want a say in the type of trees or shrubs to be used to achieve the aims of the scheme or you might be worried that planting could itself harm your property, perhaps by overshadowing your house or garden. A succinct email or letter is probably the best way to get your message across to the planning officer and you can follow that up with a phone call to make sure it has.

You can also see that the developer complies with the approved application drawings although, clearly, you do not have the right to march onto the site and start taking measurements. If works commence in advance of conditions being approved or if the works appear to be departing from approved plans, such as removing trees that are supposed to be retained or building something taller than anticipated, contact the council's enforcement section immediately. If you are concerned about breaches of condition, provide the council with evidence. For example, when building works cause a nuisance because they take place outside the working hours stipulated in a condition, keep a diary of dates and times. Back that up with timed and dated photographs, if you can, showing activity on the site at unsocial hours.

Remember this

Check that planning conditions and approved plans are adhered to.

Just because an application is approved does not mean the development will go ahead. Sometimes developers 'bank' a planning permission and seek to secure additional development by applying for something more. For instance, permission might be granted for ten houses, following which, the developer goes back and applies for twelve. It can be difficult for planners to resist incremental increases in the scale or scope of a development, so remain alert for reapplications, even where permission is granted.

Permission refused

Where planning permission is refused, look at the decision notice to see what reasons have been given for the decision. It could be that the application was refused for reasons aligned with your particular objections but equally your concerns might not feature. In particular, think about whether the reasons for refusal could be overcome by an amended scheme. This might happen where the objections are to some detail of a scheme, such as the design or materials, rather than the principle. In the former situation it is quite possible that an applicant would try to address the reasons for refusal and resubmit a revised application. In certain circumstances, applicants get a 'free go', in terms of the council's application fee, if they reapply within 12 months of the decision, so generally negotiations with the council and a resubmission occur within that time frame.

Right of appeal

The refusal of planning permission carries with it the right of appeal, as described in Chapter 4. In England and Wales appeals against refusals of householder applications must be made within twelve weeks of the decision and, for other applications, the period is normally six months. In Scotland, the period is three months for all appeals and, in Northern Ireland, it is six months. Note that there is no scope for objectors to comment further on householder appeals, although objections made against any type of application are taken into account by the appeal inspector. Anyone who objected to a planning application should be informed of an appeal. Except for householder appeals, they are provided with the appropriate reference and details of where to send any additional comments and the date by which those must be received. Be aware that time limits are applied strictly in appeals and submitting your objection a day after the deadline is likely to mean it will not be considered.

Remember this

You can contribute to all planning appeals apart from householder appeals.

Keep in mind that an applicant can appeal and reapply for planning permission at the same time, so do not assume that, since an appeal is running, there will not be a further application as well. Be aware, too, that applicants can appeal against conditions. Permission could be granted subject to conditions that the applicant finds unacceptable, perhaps restrictions on opening hours for a club or restaurant or a limit on the uses that can place on various parts of a site. In these situations, the restrictive condition could be appealed with a view to either amending it or removing it altogether.

Appeals against refusal of permission are likely where the principle of a proposal has been rejected or where the council does not support the scale of the development or, in the case of housing proposals, the number of houses proposed. As a general rule, the larger the scale of the development, the greater the chance of an appeal, if the application is refused. You should also anticipate an appeal where an application has been recommended for approval by the planning officers but turned down by the planning committee.

Most appeals are decided by the written representation method in which you have the opportunity to contribute to the appeal via a letter or statement. Any application objection is seen by the inspector considering the appeal but you might have additional points to make in light of the council's reasons for refusal and the grounds for appeal given by the appellant (the person who appeals). The appellant's full grounds of appeal have to be submitted at the start of the appeal process. You should be able to view them on your council's website or, failing that, at the council's planning department. Appellants can also submit a statement(s) in support of the appeal. For larger schemes, expect a lengthy, formal and technical-looking document prepared by a planning consultant and similar statements from other specialists. At its heart, the planning statement is likely to address each reason for refusal, or perhaps the central issues arising from those reasons. It is also likely to analyse the consistency of the proposed development with local and national planning policies.

Do not try to emulate the sort of statement prepared by a planning professional. It is better to focus on your main points of concern but do scour the appellant's statements for significant mistakes and bring any you find to the inspector's attention. Set out any local knowledge you have that is pertinent to the development, such as traffic issues, flooding or a lack of facilities. Inspectors always come from outside the area and the only information they are likely to have of the site and its surroundings is what is presented to them in the application and appeal documents, along with what they see at their brief site visit. For example, an appellant might assert that the road adjoining the appeal site is quiet and it might be quiet at the time of the site visit. But, if you know that at certain times of the day it is busy or congested, this could easily escape the inspector's attention, unless you bring it up.

As well as setting out your objections, if you would like the appeal inspector to look at the appeal site from your property when he or she makes the site inspection, say so in your letter or statement. Taking up your request is at the discretion of the inspector but most will agree.

Remember this

You can ask the appeal inspector to view the site from your property.

In England, objections have to be submitted within five weeks of the start date of the appeal. That is also the date by which the council must submit its case. Consequently, you are unlikely to be able to see the council's statement before you submit yours. In Scotland, Wales and Northern Ireland the timing varies with the type of appeal, but anyone who writes at the application stage is notified of the appeal and told the date by which any further representations have to be made. The council's statement generally fleshes out the reasons for refusal and rebuts points made in the appellant's grounds of appeal or statement. The council is also obliged to set out conditions that it would like the inspector to impose, should the appeal succeed. This is obligatory and not indicative of any weakening of the council's position. To help draw up your objection, you can speak to the planning officer to find out what the core elements of the council's case might be or what weaknesses they perceive in the appellant's case. Alternatively, the officer's report on the planning application should provide useful background on the reasons for refusal and insight into the officer's thinking. Do not simply repeat what the officer's report or reasons for refusal say but do include such evidence as you have which supports the council's arguments. If your main grievances are not reflected in the reasons for refusal, do not be deterred from including them in your objection.

As well as requesting the inspector to look at the appeal site from your property, you can also attend the visit. For written appeals, you are not allowed to make representations and the appellant does not have to let you onto private land. You can, though, point out physical things to the inspector that you want him or her to take into account. There is a fine line between pointing out something and making a point and inspectors are generally somewhat more tolerant of members of the public crossing that line, than council or appellants' representatives. So, for example, if you want to draw the inspector's attention to a particular tree due to be felled you might refer to it as the tree to be cut down which currently prevents overlooking of your bedroom window. The inspector probably would not tolerate any greater explanation of how and why overlooking might occur. Accordingly, do not view the site visit as an opportunity to get your arguments across or to lobby the inspector, as neither is likely to be allowed.

HEARING

Some appeals, especially larger or more complex proposals, are decided by means of a hearing or a public inquiry (see Chapter 4). In either case, you can attend and speak. These events are usually held at the council offices or in a local hall.

A hearing is a relatively informal process run by an inspector who will ask members of the public attending whether they have anything they want to say. This is often done early on in the hearing, to avoid members of the public having to sit through sometimes lengthy proceedings. If you do choose to speak, the inspector might ask you questions but will not allow the appellant or the council to question you directly. Inspectors vary in their willingness to include objectors in the general discussion, as opposed to simply giving a statement of their concerns.

Hearing procedure involves the inspector circulating a list of main points for discussion. He or she then asks the appellant and council for their opinions on each of the points. Members of the public might be asked for their views on each point as well, although this depends on the number in attendance and how tight the timetable is to get the hearing complete in the allotted time. The site visit can be undertaken as an extension of the hearing itself, in other words, the discussion can continue on site. This can give objectors the opportunity to explain their concerns to the inspector in situ, which can be helpful.

PUBLIC INQUIRY

A public inquiry is a much more formal process, where the council and appellant exchange statements, known as 'proofs of evidence', in advance of the inquiry. At the inquiry, each side has the opportunity to call witnesses, present their evidence and cross-examine the other side on their evidence. It is common for solicitors, barristers and specialist professional witnesses to be involved. While members of the public do not have an absolute right to speak at inquiries, in practice inspectors usually allow contributions from the public. Be aware that you might be cross-examined on your evidence, so ensure the points you make are robust and that you are prepared to have your opinions questioned. For large-scale developments, inquiries can last for several days or even weeks. Always attend the start of an inquiry, when the inspector sets out the procedure and timetable, and asks members of the public whether they wish to speak. As with hearings, inquiries can continue on site, so you might have a further opportunity at the site visit to get your points across.

With public inquiries, there is also an opportunity to be included as a main party to the appeal, along with the council and appellant, enabling you to call witnesses and cross-examine other parties. In England and Wales this is known as 'Rule 6' status and you have to apply to the Planning Inspectorate early in the appeal process asking for this status to be granted. You should indicate that you have something to bring to the inquiry that is not covered by the council or appellant's cases. If you are granted Rule 6 status, you will be expected to submit a proof(s) of evidence and will be provided with copies of the main party's proofs in advance of the inquiry. Particularly if the subject of the inquiry is a large-scale development, you should think carefully about whether it is prudent to get involved without the assistance of a planning consultant, planning solicitor or barrister.

APPEAL COSTS

The costs of participating in an appeal (known as 'expenses' in Scotland) are usually paid by the parties themselves but, in exceptional circumstances, costs can be awarded against objectors, particularly where they have Rule 6 status at an inquiry. For example, if you were to ask the inspector to look at the appeal site from your property, then fail to turn up to let him or her in, necessitating a second site visit, you might be liable for the costs of the parties attending the additional visit. Also, were you to have Rule 6 status and raise a technical argument, necessitating the appellant to commission specialist advice, which turns out to be spurious, this could lead to an award of costs against you. Cost claims are made by the main parties and the inspector decides whether costs should be awarded. However, in England the inspector has the power to grant an award without a claim being made.

Key idea

There are circumstances in which an award of costs can be made against an objector.

APPEAL DECISIONS

For all methods of appeal, the decision comes in the form of a letter in which the inspector defines what he or she sees as the main issues in the appeal and sets out his or her findings on each of those issues. It is important to read the appeal decision carefully. If the appeal is dismissed (permission refused), the decision letter spells out why. Sometimes appeals are dismissed on points of detail but the inspector makes clear that the principle of the development is acceptable. In these situations, expect a new application to be made, addressing the inspector's concerns. Where an inspector rejects some of the council's reasons for refusal, on a subsequent application, the council would be highly likely to go along with the inspector's opinion. When an appeal is allowed (permission granted), it will be subject to conditions. Should any of those conditions require further approvals (such as approval of materials or finishes), that matter will be dealt with by the council and not the inspector.

Enforcement appeals

The same opportunities exist to make representations during an enforcement appeal as with a planning appeal against refusal of permission. An enforcement notice has to be served on everyone with a legal interest in the land. It must specify the breach of planning control the council thinks has taken place, say what needs to be done about it and give a period of time to take that action. An important difference between planning and enforcement appeals is that, with the latter, the appeal can only be made on a number of pre-defined grounds. These are:

▶ Planning permission should be granted for what is alleged in the enforcement notice.

▶ The breach of planning control alleged has not occurred as a matter of fact.

- There has not been a breach of planning control.

- At the time the enforcement notice was issued it was too late to take enforcement action.

- The notice was not properly served on everyone with a legal interest in the land.

- The steps required by the enforcement notice are excessive.

- The time given to comply with the notice is too short.

An appellant in an enforcement appeal must rely on one or more of the prescribed grounds and one or more grounds can be relied on without prejudice to others. Each ground must be backed up by a statement of facts. Facts are often crucial to the case, for example, whether an activity has taken place for long enough to render it lawful (see Chapter 2) or whether an alleged breach of planning control has actually occurred. Consequently, enforcement appeals are more likely to be decided by a public inquiry than are planning appeals, as this allows evidence to be given under oath. If you attend and speak at an enforcement appeal where facts are in dispute, be prepared for your contribution to be made under oath, so be certain about the facts you rely on and have sound evidence to back them up.

With enforcement cases it is important to focus on the harm caused by the breach of planning control and not to dwell just on the fact that development went ahead without permission or that there might be some technical breach of planning law. From an objector's point of view, the advantage of an enforcement appeal is that it should be easier to demonstrate that harm is actually occurring, rather than, with planning applications and appeals, speculating about what harm might arise. The effects of a noisy, smelly or otherwise anti-social use should be self-evident, if the development is genuinely having an adverse impact. Similarly, detriment resulting from building works, such as the structure being unsightly and out of character, or a building taking away light or outlook, should be evident to any observer. However obvious the harm might be, it is still important to spell out clearly in your objection what it is, who or what is affected by it, and where and when it occurs.

Key idea

In an enforcement appeal, focus on the harm caused by the breach of planning control, rather than the breach itself.

When an enforcement appeal fails, the enforcement notice then takes effect. Be aware of the timescales within which action is required. These are set out in the enforcement notice, together with details of what has to be done, such as an activity ceasing or a building being demolished. You can monitor compliance and tip off the council should the requirements of the notice not be followed correctly.

If an enforcement appeal succeeds, check which grounds apply. Where the appeal results in the grant of planning permission, it will be subject to conditions. Should the requirements of the notice be considered excessive, the inspector will modify them to make them less onerous. As with a planning application appeal decision, it is worth reading the whole decision letter to see whether there might be scope for what was enforced against to continue or perhaps for a planning application to be made.

Legal challenges

Where an appeal is upheld and permission granted, it is possible to challenge the decision in the High Court. A challenge must be lodged within six weeks of the appeal decision. Normally such challenges are made by the council but it is possible for objectors to initiate the process, particularly if they have been closely involved in the appeal process. Challenges can only be made on legal grounds and do not directly address the inspector's decision. What can be questioned is the procedure adopted by the body which administered the appeal or the inspector (or reporter in Scotland or commissioner in Northern Ireland), and whether the inspector acted within his or her authority. Where you think an appeal decision should be challenged, speak first to the council to see whether it is considering legal action. If not, you should speak to a planning lawyer who can advise on whether there might be a case to make. It goes without saying that the costs and risks of mounting a challenge are high. The various appeal bodies in the UK are careful to carry out their procedures and decision making properly and within the law. Only a tiny percentage, less than 1 per cent, of appeal decisions are challenged and of those only 20 to 30 per cent succeed. Where a challenge is successful, the appeal goes back to be reconsidered by an inspector. A successful challenge could do no more than delay a development, as there is no guarantee that a second inspector would come to a different decision from the first.

Judicial review

In addition to the High Court challenge procedure, in exceptional circumstances, where planning permission has been granted, it might be possible to get the decision quashed (overturned) by judicial review. This applies to appeal decisions as well as council decisions. If you think a decision has been taken unlawfully, take legal advice on whether there is genuinely a case to be made. Bear in mind that a decision quashed on some procedural technicality would be reconsidered by the council or a planning inspector, who might well come to the same decision as before.

Complaints

If you are aggrieved by a decision of the council, or the actions of planning officers or councillors, you can make a formal complaint, alleging maladministration. Unfortunately, a complaint would not change the council's decision on a planning application. Likely outcomes range from an apology, or an undertaking to amend the council's procedures, through to financial compensation. Complaints are dealt with initially by the council but, in the event they are not resolved, are passed to the Ombudsman to consider. The Local Government Ombudsman deals with complaints in England and elsewhere they are dealt with by the Scottish Public Services Ombudsman, the Public Services Ombudsman for Wales and the Northern Ireland Ombudsman. The Ombudsman can find that maladministration has occurred but can only make recommendations on the remedies the council should take, including whether and how much compensation should be paid.

Focus points

* Check conditions, and ensure the developer complies with them and the approved drawings.
* Watch for re-applications after approval or refusal of permission.
* Look out for appeals after a planning application decision.
* Make representations on an appeal in accordance with the procedures.
* Get advice on legal challenges to planning approvals.

Taking it further

BOOKS

How to Design and Plan a House or Extension, George Baxter (Ovolo Books Ltd., 2013) Unravels the design process, giving a step-by-step approach to enable you to form your own design ideas and judge those of the professionals.

Housebuilder's Bible 10, Mark Brinkley (Ovolo Books Ltd., 2013) The definitive price book for all residential building projects from extensions to new builds. Contains construction insider tips. Updated yearly.

Building Your Own Home, David Snell (18th edn, Ebury Press, 2006) Covers every aspect of the house-building process, from finding opportunities, finance, to design, construction and finishes.

How to Find and Buy a Building Plot, Roy Speer and Mike Dade (3rd edn, Ovolo Books, 2010) Covers everything from defining your requirements, through finding land on or off market to assessing potential and negotiating your purchase. A complete guide.

How to Get Planning Permission, Roy Speer and Mike Dade (4th edn, Ovolo Books Ltd., 2009) Detailed guide through all the steps involved in making an application, explaining how to maximize your chances of success.

How to Stop and Influence Planning Permission, Roy Speer and Mike Dade (3rd edn, Stonepound, 2001) Comprehensive advice on having an effective voice in the planning system and insight into the most controversial types of development.

WEBSITES

ePlanning (Scotland): eplanning.scotland.gov.uk
Website for submitting on-line applications in Scotland.

Northern Ireland Planning Portal: www.planningni.gov.uk
Provides information on all aspects of the planning system in Northern Ireland.

Planning Portal: www.planningportal.gov.uk
Government website that gives information on planning applications, and facilitates on-line submission of applications in England and Wales.

Scottish Government (planning): www.scotland.gov.uk/Topics/built-environment/planning
Information about the planning system in Scotland.

Index